*Flesh of Steel*

# Flesh of Steel

LITERATURE AND THE MACHINE
IN AMERICAN CULTURE

*Thomas Reed West*

VANDERBILT UNIVERSITY PRESS

Copyright © 1967 by
VANDERBILT UNIVERSITY PRESS
Composed and printed in the
United States of America by
Heritage Printers, Inc.,
Charlotte, North Carolina
Bound by Kingsport Press, Inc.
Kingsport, Tennessee
Library of Congress
Catalogue card number
67–13997
Standard Book Number 8265–1092–2

*Second Printing 1969*

*To*
*my parents*
*and to*
*A. L. B.*

# Acknowledgments

FOR a tolerance and generosity that they balanced with an exacting criticism, I am indebted to Professors Richard Hofstadter and Robert Cross of Columbia University, who read the manuscript closely; and to Professors Herman Ausubel, Eric McKitrick, and Walter Metzger of Columbia, who advised me at various stages of the work.

I have another kind of debt so diffuse and extensive that I do not expect adequately to acknowledge it. From among my acquaintances at the time I was at work on the study I received help in many ways and degrees: in textual criticism, in discussion, in a moral support that I hope was mutually given and returned among us. I cannot name all those who contributed to the total experience, and therefore will confine myself arbitrarily to mention of some who undertook criticism of my ideas or my composition. These would be Professors David Burner of Oakland University, Alden T. Vaughan of Columbia, and Marvin Weinbaum of the University of Illinois; and Lowell Dyson, Bernard Eisenberg, Robert Fridlington, Roger Goldstein, Richard Kostelanetz, George Lankevich, John Lundoff, Paul Maloy, Leo Schelbert, and Sydney and Michael Weinberg at Columbia. And it is through the intellectual sensitivity and conversation of Patrick McCloskey, at the University of California, that I was led to an initial interest in the themes I pursue.

Finally, a separate and special mention is due to Professor Charles Gillispie of Princeton University. Having already endured with great kindness an early attempt of mine, he undertook a thorough and invaluable critique of the present study.

For permission to quote from their works, I wish to thank John Dos Passos, Waldo Frank, and Lewis Mumford. I am grateful to Mrs. Eleanor Anderson, Charles F. Adams, and Michael Lewis and to the firms of Harcourt, Brace and World and the Viking Press for permissions covering extensive quoted materials.

T. R. W.

# *Preface*

WHEN Henry Ford initiated his automotive assembly line, he established not only a method of manufacture but a kind of intellectual and literary convention. For the assembly line has come to represent the machine process itself, as a distinctive ordering of the personality: it is Discipline perfectly embodied. There are sophistication and purity in the control that it imposes. It has little to do with the cruder forms of physical hardship or economic necessity—by a happy symbolic coincidence, the assembly line and the five-dollar day made an almost simultaneous appearance in the Ford industry; rather, the line seizes upon the more cerebral and nervous faculties of the worker, and bends these to its refined pattern. An economy ever more closely meshed, a more intricate technology for office, factory plant, and laboratory, a pace and rhythm of the city street resonant of the rhythm of the factory, and, throughout, a paradoxical blending of monotony and minutely integrated complexity—here, rather than in the mines or the sweated workshops of an earlier industrial era, the discipline of the machine now holds its sway.

While industrial society bears unmistakably the character of discipline, it assumes another character equally distinct, perhaps to be designated most inclusively as a character of energy: power, massiveness, multiplicity of social and technical institutions, extravagance of productivity; and this energy may present itself in forms that contrast sharply to the discipline of technology. The contrast maintains itself even as symbolism. In the architecture of functionalism and of the skyscraper, and in its own design, the machine exhibits a disciplined crispness of line, an exactness and an intricacy of structure, and a cold brilliance of metallic surfaces; in a symbol of energy—let us say, an American city when it is seen through the eyes of a Carl Sandburg—line dissolves into bulk, rigor and delicacy of construction give way to a visible fragmentation and a clash of massive discordancies, and the coolness or glitter of finished steel is blurred in smoke and dust. And since the mechanical environment presents itself both as a concrete social condition and as a symbol, its energies and its disciplines may be said to exist on several psychic levels: in the technical intellect that creates it; in the mind and emotion that are driven by its urges, or schooled in its precisions, or strained by its pace and scope; and in the artistic and literary sensitivity that observes it as symbolism. Finally, the discipline and the energy of the machine are in unity as well as polarity, each lending to the other something of itself and its consequence: the urgency of the industrial world is a circumstance both of its energy and its disciplined pace, and complexity is at either pole.

Although the bulk of this volume is concerned with expository treatment of a number of American writings, it is not to be taken as a literary study. Its subject is the machine, and machine civilization, in the two characters of discipline and energy—their contrast, and their intricate interplay; it pursues its themes through literary exposition because certain sorts of literary temperament have reacted in a peculiarly sensitive and, of course, a peculiarly explicit and vocal manner to the phenomena with which I want to deal. I might have gotten at my themes through writings predominantly sociological or psychological (in fact, I do employ one sociologist, Thorstein Veblen), but I feel considerably safer and on far more familiar ground among the authors I have chosen, and for the purpose here they should be sufficient: they will aid in the identification of cultural moods the ultimate extent and implication of which might go beyond the compass of any study. Indeed, it may be said that when we examine the literature of the machine we encounter the machine itself, at one of its points of contact with the human consciousness; for in the categories I have defined, the machine is an event of consciousness.

The unity is purely thematic. My choice of authors has been, in a sense, quite arbitrary; while all the authors of whom major use is made are American, and all are contemporary to this century, they represent no single literary or intellectual movement, and certainly no single genre: they are Sherwood Anderson, Waldo Frank, John Dos Passos, Sinclair Lewis, Carl Sandburg, Lewis Mumford, Veblen, and Harold Stearns. These authors have been chosen because collectively their works sketch in unusual clarity and elaboration the states of the machine that I have designated by the terms "discipline" and "energy." The themes dominate the textual analysis itself which follows, not the main drift or the more general literary significance of each author's work, but points originally intended, perhaps, to be wholly secondary—in so far as they were directly intended at all. The chapters are arranged on a similar principle: the reader will thus discover that Veblen and Sandburg go together, as do Mumford and Stearns. All this is not to say that my selection either of writers or of motifs is unrepresentative. Certainly, the themes are common enough to literature: the machine-as-repression is close to being a cliché; but I have chosen and ordered my materials to the end that the cultural properties and their polarity will stand clean.

Within the rigid thematic structure, however, it is necessary to follow the argument of the authors in considerable narrative detail, for their contribution to the study lies precisely in their ability to exhibit the machine in its qualitative nuance. To this part of the analysis I have brought as much impartiality as I could manage. For example, the predominant literary sentiment toward the discipline of the machine has been one of lament, and it is the typical, if not the only, sentiment among the works I examine; for me, to the contrary, those disciplines suggest an ascetic strength rather than a cultural decline: but I have reported the attitude and argument of the writings fairly carefully, trusting that in emphasizing the severities of the machine they have made it all the more possible to recognize its stern virtues. Each of my authors wrote, not only in response to his social and technological environment, but in response to literary traditions and to his private and perhaps unique concerns. In my introductory remarks to each writer I have given something of the personal perspective from which he viewed his culture.

The machine itself is the nucleus of the inquiry. Surrounding this nucleus is the larger range of industrial society—its peculiar productive and social forces, its special technique, its distinctive orderings of men and materials; and of all these the machine is in part basis, in part analogue. Complication and minuteness are equally attributes of a precisioned mechanical structure and the structure of finance; the strategy of a commuter who must adapt himself to the flow of subway traffic compares with the strategy of a worker at the assembly line or that of a producer before the flow of materials and finished goods— or a member of a liberal profession in face of an expanding complexity of information; the force and body of a corporation correspond aesthetically to the weight and force of empowered steel. One of the writers to be discussed, Sinclair Lewis, concerned himself hardly at all with the machine, yet his interpretation of the American business-man and industrialist brings him within the theme of the study. And in fact the themes point even beyond the scope of industrialism, for a number of direct connections and suggestive analogies may be drawn between the authors' views of the machine and their views of other elements in the American heritage: the disciplines of "Puritan"—much-abused word—morality, the energies of democracy, of our continent and soil. The dualism of the machine is revealed as a type and incident in a more extensive polarity within the national experience.

Though the study examines the work of only a few authors, the themes in their broadest application may be detected, in varying forms and combinations, throughout a considerable portion of recent American literature. We encounter an American energy in the savagely potent land of William Carlos Williams's *In the American Grain*; in the American continent that commanded the imagination of Thomas Wolfe—a continent of such size that its sojourners cannot possess it, but must hurl themselves over it in a frenzy of hunger, or build some sort of refuge against its loneliness; energy in the new and empty earth, the toughness and the immensities of the American land in the poetry of Archibald MacLeish; in the broad tamed prairies of Willa Cather's *O Pioneers!* There is energy in the American character, generous and careless, as it is set forth by the young Ezra Pound's *Patria Mia*; in the vigor and potency of John Steinbeck's American folk; in the mixture of ethnic stocks and the turbulent industrial environment that confronted the immigrant Louis Adamic. The disciplines of American society take form as the Puritan constraints that have often been the prey of American authors—Williams is again an example; the regimentations of modern society against which E. E. Cummings has done battle; the abstract universals of science, for which John Crowe Ransom would have us substitute a disciplined sensitivity to the particular and concrete.[1]

Three additional explanatory remarks are in order. Though my main interest is in comparatively recent writers who have had knowledge of a fully sophisticated technology and could build upon a fairly well established literary tradition of industrialism, the opening chapter explores the themes through discussion of some earlier

---

1. It should be clear that the polarity of which I treat is only one of several that gain definition in American literature. In *The Machine in the Garden: Technology and the Pastoral Ideal in America* (New York: Oxford University Press, 1964), Leo Marx discovers a broader dualism within which the elements of mine might be encompassed: the land, as innocence and harmony, invaded by the civilized complexities and aggressions that are epitomized in the machine—and there the machine may represent both disciplined repression and massive disorder.

authors. And because the restraints and the compulsions of the machine possess so extensive a moral significance of their own, two of the chapters, VI and VII, turn aside from consideration of the discipline-energy dualism with which much of the volume deals and examine some relatively favorable views of the machine, and the American business temperament, in their disciplines alone. Finally, I must acknowledge the inadequacy of the word "machine." In a century that conceptually dissolves the material world as we had known it, replaces levers and steam with electrical and nuclear power, and moves from mechanics to cybernetics, "machine" with its almost muscular connotation begins to have an archaic sound; and although this was not so much the case even as recently as a few decades ago when most of my writers were at work, they too were dealing, consciously or not, with a technology more and more un-"mechanical." I hope that the word will be taken as a shorthand for the designation of phenomena many of which advance beyond that of mechanization itself.

# Contents

*Flesh of Steel*

# Chapter 1

# *"The Shapes Arise"*

THE machine proves itself increasingly fecund not only in the economic goods but in its own symbolism. Its twentieth-century forms—the assembly line, the power plant, the skyscraper, the automobile, even the wrist watch, at once dictatorial and fastidiously unobtrusive—connote with striking effectiveness the extent of its control over society and the meticulousness of that control. The symbolism is endless: it is inherent in the closer fusion of the factory with the higher sciences; in the transformation of city traffic into a function of the machine, its inner motions rhythmically meshed like those within an engine or a factory room; in a new polish of surfaces, a diffusion of light, and a pure line that Lewis Mumford, in *Technics and Civilization*, has held to characterize the latest, "neotechnic" stage of industrialism. Quite possibly, machine sketches of the sort that are to be found in the work of Sherwood Anderson could not have been drawn a century ago; there is too much cool light, too many fine precise lines and harmonies in the factories and technological minds he portrayed: the shy inventor Hugh McVey in the novel *Poor White,* or the craftsmanlike technicians and delicate factory machinery of *Perhaps Women.*

But if the steam-and-smoke mechanics and the looser meshings of industry in the Victorian age provided only an imperfect imagery of the discipline to which the machine might attain over itself and over men, the discipline and its imagery were present. In his *Capital,* Marx was able to expound at length upon the division of labor and the subservience of the laborer to the speed and uniformities of the factory.[1] Well before the present century, of course, literature had come to strike a series of elaborate postures toward its mechanical surroundings, and the twentieth-century writer has had an opportunity to draw upon these, as well as upon the technological sophistication of his own immediate environment. The works of Thomas Carlyle, Charles Dickens, John Ruskin, Walt Whitman, and Henry Adams give some clues to the impressions that the machine was making upon the consciousness of the nineteenth and early twentieth centuries, and of what might be handed on, by way of intellectual inheritance, to writers of more recent decades.

" 'Coal and iron, so long close unregardful neighbours, are wedded together; Birmingham and Wolverhampton, and the hundred Stygian forges, with their fire-throats, and never-resting sledge-hammers, rose into day,' " wrote Car-

1. *Capital, the Communist Manifesto and Other Writings,* edited, with an introduction, by Max Eastman (New York: Random House, The Modern Library, 1932), pp. 78, 85, 115–128.

lyle in "Chartism," an essay of 1839.[2] In this manner the industrial era presented itself to Carlyle. It was an affair of Stygian forges and fire-throats, a thrust of Saxon energy turned to the subduing of iron and cotton; it was a more perfect expression of an eternal work-ethic, and even a heightened application of intelligence to the act of labor— but never, or at least not typically, did machine industry appear in Carlyle's writings as a totally new method, a new habit of minute calculation, a timed pace of work or the complete subjugation of the individual and his skill to the demands of a machine.

It was a vision of the industrial age consistent with Carlyle's roughhewn perception of things. Philosophically, he saw existence as a surge and fusion of forces, whether the crude power of physical nature or the purer force of Christianity; visually, he grasped scenes and events in their rougher lines and dominant colors, in great blocks and chunks; morally, he admired directness, honesty in the confronting of existence, and despised subtlety and facile wit. Hence, the hero or prophet is strong, Carlyle thought, in the *force* rather than the cleverness of his insight; in the plainness and sincerity with which he fronts the universe and lets it teach its truths to him.[3] And while Carlyle conceived of the task of man as one of ordering the still untamed element of existence ("Wheresoever thou findest Disorder, there is thy eternal enemy; attack him swiftly, subdue him; make Order of him, the subject not of Chaos, but of Intelligence, Divinity and Thee!"),[4] order never seemed to signify a nicety of proportion—it was, rather,

2. *The Works of Thomas Carlyle* (Centenary Edition; New York: Charles Scribner's Sons, 1898–1901), XXIX, 185.

3. *On Heroes, Hero-Worship and the Heroic in History* (1841), in *Works*, V, 45, 54.

4. *Past and Present* (1843), in *Works*, X, 201.

the kind of order that the form of a great shaggy mountain fixes upon broken rock.

The gigantic energies and bold shapes of the industrial age therefore would have for Carlyle their appeal, and industrialism would be for him essentially a phenomenon of force, needing only to be freed from its bondage to Mammon to fulfill its destiny.

> "The Saxon kindred burst forth into cotton-spinning, cloth-cropping, iron-forging, steamengineing, railwaying, commercing and careering towards all the winds of Heaven,—in this inexplicable noisy manner; the noise of which, in Power-mills, in progress-of-the-species Magazines, still deafens us somewhat. Most noisy, sudden!"[5]

Industrialism did appear to Carlyle a moral discipline, but no different in kind from all other labors and disciplines whereby a man gets into a true relationship with Force, and an honest relationship with the laws of existence that must be obeyed in the act of work. He wrote in *Past and Present* (1843):

> The grim inarticulate veracity of the English people, unable to speak its meaning in words, has turned itself silently on things; and the dark powers of Material Nature have answered, "Yes, this at least is true, this is not false!"

The labors of England were "the one God's Voice we have heard in these two atheistic centuries."[6] So we cannot look to Carlyle to furnish any detailed account of the methods of industry, or of the more minute adjustments, mental and physical, that the machine might force upon its servants. Instead, he demonstrates how the rougher and more striking images to which industrialism gives form might

5. "Chartism," in *Works*, XXIX, 184.
6. *Works*, X, 168–169.

impress themselves upon the consciousness of its observers and provides a contrast to those writers who would inquire more closely into the nature of industrialism as a specific technique and discipline.

Yet while Carlyle seldom concerned himself with the technique of industry, he did see in the machine one potential danger to the human spirit—a danger posed not so much by the machine itself and the order of labor and life it brings about as by the sterile analogies and false lessons to which it could give rise. Carlyle complained of the utilitarian and rationalistic philosophies, the corrupted uses of science that would measure and dissect existence by logic alone and hold the universe a machine and the human soul a weighing balance for pleasure and pain. These philosophies meant the denial of wonder, the devitalization of thought and experience[7]—the machine become a symbol not of life-force but of spiritual death.

In a single novel of Dickens, the reader is brought concretely into the smoky industrial world that Carlyle viewed only in its more general massive outline. Like other novels of Dickens, *Hard Times* (1854) is at once a bit of extravagant and romantic characterization and a work of social criticism. But there is about it a rather unexpected austerity; the narrative is relatively short and very much to the point, there is little fatness and ruddiness of descriptive detail, the social message is stark and direct. And in its analysis of industrialism as a social force and as a repressive discipline of the human personality, *Hard Times* is strikingly modern.[8]

The novel analyzes mid-nineteenth century industrialism

7. *Sartor Resartus* (1833), in *Works*, I, 53–54; *Heroes*, in *Works*, V, 20–21, 76; "Signs of the Times" (1829), in *Works*, XXVII, 56–82.

8. See the introduction by John H. Middendorf in *Hard Times* (New York: Harper and Brothers, 1960), pp. v–xx.

in its two complementary and mutually illustrative forms—physical and intellectual. Materially, the industrial system resides in Coketown, a murky inferno of monotonous, unending factory labor, monotonous streets, grim uniformity. Intellectually, it resides in the Gradgrind household, where children are brought up on Fact and science and utilitarian philosophy and every thought is a polemic in defense of Coketown. Coketown and Thomas Gradgrind are the closest of allies, and each is an explanation of the other.

Coketown

> had a black canal in it, and a river that ran purple with ill-smelling dye, and vast piles of building full of windows where there was a rattling and a trembling all day long, and where the piston of the steam-engine worked monotonously up and down, like the head of an elephant in a state of melancholy madness.

Streets were similar; days were all alike. "These attributes of Coketown were in the main inseparable from the work by which it was sustained. . . . "[9] The Coketown thread of the novel is a tale, dreary as its setting, of an honest mill-hand burdened with a drunken wife, persecuted by his employer—the blustering "self-made" Bounderby—and ostracized by his fellow workers, a victim finally of a mine accident. And while the laborers of Coketown are seen to struggle under all the conventionally recognizable forms of economic oppression, Dickens did not set forth their problem simply or even primarily as one of poverty or child labor or industrial hazard, but as a spiritual starvation.

Against the story of Coketown Dickens played the story of the Gradgrind family. Here individualist industrialism and political economy can find their spokesman in the utilitarian dogmatist, Thomas Gradgrind. Here also the sterile

9. *Ibid.*, pp. 28–29.

material existence of Coketown is reflected in the sterile abstractions by which Gradgrind lives, and in the scientific education given his children—trained from earliest years always to seize upon the rigid blunt Fact and never to wonder or to toy with fancy. Especially modern in its implications is Dickens's portrayal of Louisa Gradgrind, her life almost destroyed through the suppression and maiming of her human feelings; it is a psychological study suggestive of the diagnoses that post-Freudian writers would make of the repressed industrial personality. In sum, the Gradgrind philosophy and the Gradgrind system of education constitute a discipline, iron-hard and iron-cold, that clamps itself upon the mind as the factory environment settles upon the operatives.[10]

But while Dickens maintained a harmony and a correspondence between Coketown and Gradgrindism, he clearly placed the greater responsibility for the ills of industrialism at the account of the Gradgrinds and the Bounderbys, the intellectual and business representatives of the new era. Mechanism itself has its role to play—"the noon bell rang. . . . The looms, and wheels, and Hands all out of gear for an hour";[11] but there is no real suggestion that technology might be the prime mover, the self-sustained arbiter of new social forms. Other Victorian writers would attack more directly the machine, the factory, and the new technology of labor. Among the most important was John Ruskin.

In one of the essays gathered in *Unto This Last*, Ruskin wrote:

> In fact, it may be discovered that the true veins of wealth are purple—and not in Rock, but in Flesh—perhaps even that the

10. *Ibid.*, p. 32.
11. *Ibid.*, p. 92.

final outcome and consummation of all wealth is in the pro-
ducing as many as possible full-breathed, bright-eyed, and
happy-hearted human creatures.

And in the same series:

> No scene is continually and untiringly loved, but one rich
> by joyful human labour; smooth in field; fair in garden; full
> in orchard; trim, sweet, and frequent in homestead; ringing
> with voices of vivid existence.[12]

Here, as clearly as in any of Ruskin's more elaborate state-
ments of social reform, can be found the substance of his
dream for the good society. It is a vision not of a civilization
reconstructed in due accordance with scientific reform
theory, efficiently administered and economically progres-
sive, but of a society virtuous, sociable, and happy in the
concrete details of its daily life—a society of peasants and
good craftsmen; and its ultimate bond would be that of
Christian love. This grasp of the social situation is at the
heart of the argument in *Unto This Last.* For the work is
an attack upon the conventional theories of political economy; and the essence of the argument is that the liberal
economists had misdefined the true nature of wealth and,
therefore, the true means to its achievement—had failed
to see that the value of goods and services lies, not in the
price they are artifically assigned under a market economy,
but in their possibilities for the enrichment of life. From
this concrete sense of wealth stemmed all of Ruskin's more
explicit schemes for social reconstruction: for child education, for government regulation of the economy, for the
acknowledgment of kingship and class distinction.

The main force of Ruskin's social reformist argument
was therefore directed against the laissez faire economics

12. *Unto This Last* (London: G. Allen and Unwin, 1923), pp. 64–65,
167–168. The essays were first published in 1860.

of Victorian Britain, and against every institution of the nineteenth century—whether in its politics, its economics, its methods of labor, or its aesthetic—that appeared poor in earthy life-value. Specifically, he attacked the industrial disciplines of labor; for he believed that the division of labor and the demand for a mechanical perfection in workmanship eliminate all expressiveness from labor and prevent the laborer from translating his vital self into the materials he handles. The point is made with great thoroughness in one of the most famous of Ruskin's writings—the essay on "The Nature of Gothic," which appeared in the second volume of *The Stones of Venice*, published in 1853.

The essential mistake of the industrial regime, insisted Ruskin, is its requirement that every manufactured product be perfect in finish, an exact fulfillment of specifications rigidly established. But if a worker of living flesh and groping spirit is to approach such perfection, he must contradict his own imperfect nature, submerge his personality, and become a tool:

> Men were not intended to work with the accuracy of tools, to be precise and perfect in all their actions. If you will have that precision out of them, and make their fingers measure degrees like cog-wheels, and their arms strike curves like compasses, you must unhumanize them. . . . The eye of the soul must be bent upon the finger-point, and the soul's force must fill all the invisible nerves that guide it, ten hours a day, that it may not err from its steely precision, and so soul and sight be worn away. . . . On the other hand, if you will make a man of the working creature, you cannot make a tool. Let him but begin to imagine, to think, to try to do anything worth doing; and the engine-turned precision is lost at once. Out come all his roughness, all his dulness, all his incapability; shame upon shame, failure upon failure, pause after pause: but out comes the whole majesty of him also. . . .

And through the intensification, in modern times, of the division of labor, the workers themselves are atomized:

> Divided into mere segments of men—broken into small fragments and crumbs of life; so that all the little piece of intelligence that is left in a man is not enough to make a pin, or a nail, but exhausts itself in making the point of a pin, or the head of a nail.[13]

In contrast to the sterile perfection of modern workmanship Ruskin placed the grandeur of Gothic architecture.

The essay "The Nature of Gothic" is of the greatest significance. Its own influence has been considerable—most notably, perhaps, upon William Morris;[14] and it expresses a kind of objection to the industrial order that became increasingly vocal in the late nineteenth century and after—in Morris, in G. D. H. Cole and Guild Socialism, in Eric Gill. Among American novelists, Sherwood Anderson has explored with special sensitivity the antagonism between craftsmanship and the industrial method.

In "The Nature of Gothic," the industrial era comes into the sharpest focus; the meaning of the era is discovered in an examination of the factory itself and of the specific discipline the factory represents. In the work of Walt Whitman, American contemporary to Ruskin, the focus is again widened—and blurred, and we view the machine age, as Carlyle viewed it, in its larger outlines.

Material and soul, appearance and Idea, multiple and One: the Platonic dualism that the American Transcendentalists carried over, as did Carlyle, in part from Germanic metaphysics gives the philosophic clue to the poetic

13. *The Stones of Venice* (New York: John Wiley and Sons, 1888), II, 161–162, 165. Originally published in 1853.

14. For a careful appraisal of the effect of *The Stones of Venice* upon Morris, see Lloyd Wendell Eshleman, *A Victorian Rebel: The Life of William Morris* (New York: Charles Scribner's Sons, 1940), pp. 164–167.

mysticism of Whitman. On the one side stands the Whitmanesque zest for the concrete, the diverse, the vital; on the other, the assertion of a spirit that is the "ever-tending, the finalè of visible forms."[15] And this intuition suffuses the poems, so that the universe they create appears in almost kaleidoscopic motion, flinging itself momentarily apart into the most discordant hues and shapes as its substances are agitated, assuming some new quiet and harmony, only to fracture again into multiplicity.

From among the discrete and merging images that pass before the reader, a few glimpses are caught of the machine; but they are glimpses only, shifting and suggestive rather than distinct. In "To a Locomotive in Winter" (1876) the impression is of a keen and reckless force:

> *Type of the modern—emblem of motion and power—*
> *pulse of the continent,*
>
> .　.　.　.　.　.　.　.　.　.　.　.　.　.
>
> *Fierce-throated beauty!*
> *Roll through my chant with all thy lawless music,*
> *thy swinging lamps at night. . . .*[16]

In other passages, industrial activities are seen as expressions of a vast, swift-moving and creative American democracy. Here there may be no clear separation between industrial occupations and the crafts; both are revelations of a democratic impulse and belong to the phenomenal world at its most concrete, its most energetic; both are material reflections of a spirit, an American Idea. In "Song of the Broad-Axe" (1856), the axe becomes the symbol of an acting America; out of its wielding emerge the structures, physical and social and even spiritual, of American life. Yet

15. "Starting from Paumanok" (1860), in *The Complete Poetry and Prose of Walt Whitman*, with an introduction by Malcolm Cowley (New York: Pellegrini and Cudahy, 1948), I, 53.

16. *Poetry and Prose*, I, 407–408.

among these, only a few are distinctively of the order of machine industry.

> *The axe leaps!*
> *The solid forest gives fluid utterances,*
>
> . . . . . . . . . . . . . . . . . .
>
> *The shapes arise!*
> *Shapes of factories, arsenals, foundries, markets,*
> *Shapes of the two-threaded tracks of railroads,*
> *Shapes of the sleepers of bridges, vast frameworks,*
>       *girders, arches,*
> *Shapes of the fleets of barges, tows, lake and canal craft,*
>       *river craft,*
>
> . . . . . . . . . . . . . . . . . .
>
> *The main shapes arise!*
> *Shapes of Democracy total, result of centuries,*
> *Shapes ever projecting other shapes,*
> *Shapes of turbulent manly cities,*
> *Shapes of the friends and home-givers of the whole earth,*
> *Shapes bracing the earth and braced with the whole earth.*

And "Song of the Exposition" (1871) makes poetry of America's inventive and industrial activity—the material outpouring of the American soul.[17]

"Passage to India" (1868) carries a broader conception. The poem interprets the engineering labors of the modern world as representing a march toward the unity of the earth: the binding of regions and peoples through the canal, the railroad, and the cable, and the return of Western man to the Orient, the ancient. After the physical union is to come a mystic fusion of parts, and a fulfillment of the soul.[18] Finally, it is significant that Whitman discovered in some of the industrial creations of his nineteenth century the cleanliness of design that is more readily associated

17. *Ibid.*, pp. 186–204.
18. *Ibid.*, pp. 361–369.

with the industrial architecture of a later day; in the eighteen sixties he could discern "the strong light works of engineers," the "high growths of iron, slender, strong, light" that graced Manhattan.[19]

Whitman made little direct contribution to a conception of the machine: he never treated industrialism in any major or even particularly coherent manner. But indirectly his effect may have been considerable. He taught American writers to disregard traditional literary forms and to report the energy and variety of life—to look to the strong raw facts of American society and relate them to the diversity and potentiality of democracy. These predilections shaped Whitman's own understanding of American industrialism; and many a later author, celebrating the industrial force of the American Middle West or the democracy of the sky-scraper, might draw upon the Whitman heritage to strengthen the insight and invigorate the expression. The connection seems most apparent in the poems of Sandburg, with their Whitmanesque though original renderings of an imagery taken from democratic and industrial sources.

*The Education of Henry Adams* was printed privately in 1906. Adams's great autobiography might almost be considered as among the writings of main concern in this essay rather than as a precursor; it was contemporary to some of the work of Veblen and preceded by only a few years the earliest work of Frank, Anderson, and Lewis. But the *Education* can serve a more useful purpose in illustrating the continuities and discontinuities between the nine-teenth-century insights of Carlyle, Ruskin, and Whitman, and the viewpoints of the writers whose industrial milieu has been more advanced. Born in 1838, Adams was fully a Victorian—or even, so he thought, an anachronism out of

19. "Passage to India," in *ibid.*, p. 361; "Mannahatta" (1860), in *ibid.*, p. 409.

the colonial period—and was therefore a historian, not only of the industrial conditions of the twentieth century, but of rapid industrial change; the philosophy he expounded in the *Education* represents an immediate intellectual reaction to the new sciences of energy which by the turn of the century were revising the mechanical physics of the past; the entire tone of the work conveys an impression of an industrial civilization quickened in its tempo, more completely expressive of mammoth resistless energies than was the society of Carlyle and Whitman, or of Adams's own earlier years.

The *Education* is a puzzling work and can be taken in more than one way. The ironic posture, the cutting references to politics and business suggest that possibly it is at heart simply a commentary upon the decline of the republic following the political defeat of the Adams family and the principles they had sustained. The scientific-philosophical framework upon which Adams built his narrative might then be little more than a jest, a satirical method for the measurement of an acceleration into anarchy; or it could be a bitter conviction stemming from a narrow set of concerns. Yet Adams took his historical philosophy too seriously for this and spent too much of his later life in its careful statement and application. *Mont-Saint-Michel and Chartres* (1904), his study of thirteenth-century faith and architecture, had been planned as a companion to the story of Adams's own times; together they would define two historical points from which to plot and measure scientifically the movement of force in history.[20] And in two essays of 1909 and 1910, later published by Brooks Adams in *The Degradation of the Democratic Dogma*, Henry Adams gave

20. *The Education of Henry Adams: An Autobiography* (Boston and New York: Houghton Mifflin Company, 1946), pp. 434–435. Appeared privately in 1906.

further definition to his historical philosophy. That philosophy is worth consideration; for it is inseparable from Adams's interpretation of industrialism and is in itself a testament to a new scientific era.

Adams's philosophy of history amounts to the conviction that society is no more or less than a function of physical energy and that human history repeats the tendency of all existence toward an ever-accelerated release of energy, a progression from compact force to force in diffuse complexity. Man, who seeks order, has striven again and again to control new elements of chaotic energy as they appear, to maintain against the anarchy a workable unity; but it is a fragile unity that can only be defended along a widening front. For the nineteenth century, the increase in force had expressed itself in the volume and intensity of coal power, and in the unleashing of the other great forces of industrial civilization; only recently "a new universe of force had been revealed in radiation."[21]

In the later chapters of the *Education*, Adams sketched the revolutionary developments in science, toward the last years of the nineteenth century, that had contributed to his radical interpretation of existence and of history; and in the essays published in *The Degradation of the Democratic Dogma* he buttressed his ideas with the terms and findings of the new science: the law of the dissipation of energy, the recognition that energy might exist in supersensory phases, the discovery of radium. The power of Adams's historical philosophy, however, lies not in any inherent scientific merit but in the artistic form it imparts to the *Education*. The work is a chronicle of historical movement during the lifetime of its author, from the relative stability of Adams's Boston-Quincy childhood—a little out of date even for its own time, he implied—to the anarchic upheaval of indus-

21. *Ibid.*, pp. 460–461, 490–491.

trial and social energy that confronted Adams at the beginning of the twentieth century; and by setting the historical development against a wider background of natural forces in accelerating thrust and complexity, he brought dramatic integrity and continuity to his tale and sharply intensified its feeling. Energy and multiplicity become inevitable; society assumes an irresistible motion of its own, increasing into infinity. The dramatic scheme moves to a fitting climax —in an impression of New York City in 1904:

> The outline of the city became frantic in its effort to explain something that defied meaning. Power seemed to have outgrown its servitude and to have asserted its freedom. The cylinder had exploded, and thrown great masses of stone and steam against the sky. The city had the air and movement of hysteria, and the citizens were crying, in every accent of anger and alarm, that the new forces must at any cost be brought under control. Prosperity never before imagined, power never yet wielded by man, speed never reached by anything but a meteor, had made the world irritable, nervous, querulous, unreasonable and afraid. All New York was demanding new men, and all the new forces, condensed into corporations, were demanding a new type of man—a man with ten times the endurance, energy, will and mind of the old type—for whom they were ready to pay millions at sight. As one jolted over the pavements or read the last week's newspapers, the new man seemed close at hand, for the old one had plainly reached the end of his strength, and his failure had become catastrophic.[22]

In conceiving industrialism in its energy and bulk, Adams was in the company of Carlyle and of Whitman. But the energy he perceived, particularly in its twentieth-century forms, was of a nature at once subtler and more gigantic than the simple rugged force that Carlyle had depicted. It was an energy that had spilled out of the fac-

22. *Ibid.*, p. 499.

tory and overrun the whole of society; it was paced, and unimaginably complex; it issued from mysterious sub- stances and compounds unknown to the contemporaries of Carlyle; and it was uncovered, for immediate or future use, not through the crude mechanics of the earlier nineteenth century, but through science perfected to the finest edge. He had seen, said the author,

> the number of minds, engaged in pursuing force—the truest measure of its attraction—increase from a few scores or hundreds, in 1838, to many thousands in 1905, trained to sharpness never before reached, and armed with instru- ments amounting to new senses of indefinite power and ac- curacy, while they chased force into hiding-places where Nature herself had never known it to be, making analyses that contradicted being, and syntheses that endangered the elements.

The new scientific formulations, in themselves the basis of Adams's philosophy, were of the very fiber of the industrial civilization of the twentieth century as Adams saw its be- ginnings and imagined its future; they would supply its energies, train its intellect and, it seems, in the very fact of revealing the multiplicity of existence, would hurl the twentieth-century mind even further into multiplicity.[23] They would be, in effect, the intellectualization and epit- ome of twentieth-century energy, as the steam-engine had been the symbol of energy in Carlyle's day.

In still another manner, the *Education* may be contrasted to the work of Carlyle. While the Scots historian saw the machine age only in its mass and force, and Ruskin was concerned only with its disciplines, in the machine world of Adams the distinction is obliterated: energy at its most anarchic is the instrument of discipline. The tempo of the new civilization is set by its greater energies, and man ad-

23. *Ibid.*, pp. 457–458, 494–495.

justs himself to that tempo; through its own impetus, complexity begets a larger complexity, and the mind schools itself to some grasp of the expanding whole; the human personality strains and tenses in response to every new acceleration in complex energy. And despite the pessimism with which Adams viewed the future, he did not fail to respect the mind that would come to grips with the emergent forces of the twentieth century.

> At the rate of progress since 1800, every American who lived into the year 2000 would know how to control unlimited power. He would think in complexities unimaginable to an earlier mind. He would deal with problems altogether beyond the range of earlier society.

In face of a staggering expansion in natural and social energies, only an expansion in human energy, intelligence, and endurance would suffice.[24]

In the work of Carlyle, of Whitman, and of Henry Adams, industrialism appears in the form of energy; in the work of Dickens, Ruskin, and again Adams, it appears in the form of discipline. As an energy, industrialism projects itself upon a magnificent scale. It assumes weight and ruggedness of contour; all its acts are exhibitions of a massive power, wielded against massive materials. As a discipline, industrialism becomes tighter and more exacting in its method. It subjects the workman to the ordered routines of the factory and demands of his imperfect spirit a relentless perfection in labor; it drills the intellect in science and grim mechanical Fact and in the precise understanding and mastery of expanding complexities. In these forms the machine would continue to confront writers of a more recent day: its disciplines, still subtler; its energies, more multiple and swift.

24. *Ibid.*, pp. 496–497, 499.

# Chapter 2

# *Sherwood Anderson* THE MACHINE
## AND THE CRAFTSMAN'S SENSIBILITY

S HERWOOD ANDERSON can best be conceived as a "drowsing village mystic," in the words of Alfred Kazin: as an author whose work is characterized by a "certain sleepy inarticulation, a habit of staring at faces in wondering silence, a way of groping for words and people indistinguishably."[1] Frequently, Anderson would take some idea or object and not so much positively define its beauty as turn it over, speculate about it and savor of it, as though attempting to see how beautiful it might be made to appear. Something of his own method is suggested in a passage from *Dark Laughter*:

> Deep in him perhaps Bruce had always had ·buried away a kind of inner tenderness about words, ideas, moods. He had

1. *On Native Grounds: An Interpretation of Modern American Prose Literature* (New York: Reynal and Hitchcock, 1942), p. 212.

wanted to experiment, slowly, going carefully, handling words as you might precious stones, giving them a setting.[2]

Anderson's experience of things was, then, highly catholic, receptive to the immediate impression; and he urged upon his readers a similar receptivity to existence and to the senses—a receptivity that he identified with craftsmanship. In *A Story Teller's Story*, he described the love of craft as the basis for "that love of life—that with the male comes only through the love of surfaces, sensually felt through the fingers"; and in *Dark Laughter*, he wrote: "A workman, like Sponge, saw, felt, tasted things through his fingers. There was a disease of life due to men getting away from their own hands, their own bodies too."[3] From Anderson's mood sprang a number of observations that together define a polarity within the machine—on the one hand, a splendor of power and an aesthetic, and on the other, a discipline repressive of experience; and beyond, a more inclusive polarity in American civilization, concordant with the dualism of the machine.

Anderson's concern with an openness of the senses led him to distrust any force that constrains. Puritanism is one of these; industrialism is another, and for many reasons. Its technology disciplines the mind to gray facts; its pace assaults the nerves; its factories enslave the worker; its mighty and perfect machines put his manhood to shame. On the other hand, through the receptivity of Anderson's mood, his responsiveness to the lyric quality in any phenomenon, he became interested in several dramatic or poetic properties in machinery. Sometimes the qualities he found were those qualities of mass and power that we have marked in the appraisals of other writers. At these mo-

2. *Dark Laughter* (New York: Boni and Liveright, 1925), pp. 20–21.
3. *A Story Teller's Story* (New York: B. W. Huebsch, 1924), p. 81; *Dark Laughter*, p. 98.

ments, Anderson could equate the might of the machine with the might of the American land. Hence, the power of the Tennessee Valley Authority dams as he portrayed them in *Puzzled America* seems to form a unit with the water power of the land; and a description of industrial Chicago suggests the city's foundation in the abundant soil of Mid-America. In other instances, Anderson discovered in the machine a character of delicacy and ordered grace. And because Anderson appears to have responded in so similar a manner to both these aesthetics of the machine, the second of which approaches the functionalist, we shall have to set Anderson's vision slightly apart from the others with which we deal: it will be necessary to imagine a polarity in which a discipline is set in intricate relationship—even, at times, in alliance—with an element that is compounded both of massive energy and of functionalist form.

## The Machine as Discipline

While Anderson remained constant in construing as repression the institutions of Puritan, business, and industrial America, his understanding of the matter underwent considerable development in the course of his career. One of his earliest works, *Marching Men*, treats of the oppressions of industrialism in a manner notably different from those ways in which, in later writings, he was to approach the problem.

For *Marching Men* seems to accuse modern civilization of destroying the order in life by which the lyric mood is achieved, rather than of imposing upon the poetic spirit a cramped discipline. As seen in this early work, the characteristic of the American industrial world is disorder; yet it is not the splendid turmoil recorded in one of Anderson's later depictions of Chicago, but a chaos devoid of chaotic grandeur. "Chicago is one vast gulf of disorder. Here is the passion for gain, the very spirit of the bourgeoise [sic] gone drunk with desire. The result is something terrible. Chicago is leaderless, purposeless, slovenly, down at the heels."[4]

Anderson sought to describe a form of discipline that would bring poetry to the country. He pointed to the orderly, fruitful cornfields and the lesson of the fields, forgotten by Chicago. The hero of the tale, Beaut McGregor, brings one lyrical moment to American labor, when he inspires it with the idea of forming itself into a disciplined army that would march forth, not so much as a means to the achievement of any definite goal, but as an expression of itself and its latent force. McGregor's dream is of "the thunder of a million feet rocking the world and driving the great song of order purpose and discipline into the soul of Americans."[5]

The reconciliation of *Marching Men* to the rest of Anderson's writing lies in the nature of the discipline involved in the story. It is not a technological discipline, as in Anderson's later works, and unlike the discipline of technology it would not require restraint, the crushing of desire, or the submission of the mind and body to painful and lifeless processes of work. The order instilled by McGregor is quite the opposite. It is an urge rather than a denial, and it is the channeled expression of crude power and instinct. Of each worker who is caught up in McGregor's movement the novelist wrote, "Power had breathed its message into his brain. Of a sudden he saw himself as a part of a giant walking in the world."[6]

4. *Marching Men* (New York: John Lane Company; London: John Lane; Toronto: S. B. Gundy, 1917), p. 156.
5. *Ibid.*, pp. 156, 178.
6. *Ibid.*, p. 267.

It is, we find, the very lack of this manner of discipline that permits the factory to impose its own regimentation. Falling out of step with his fellows, the workman loses consciousness of his own individuality and so permits himself to be herded into a factory without complaint.[7] In *Marching Men*, as throughout Anderson's work, liberated intuition confronts the emotional constriction of American life; but here the indictment is against the destructive activity of modern America, the disruption of the beautiful and orderly arrangements of life within which the lyric mood can expand, while later writings explore the repressive new order of industrialism.

*Poor White*, which appeared only three years after *Marching Men*, analyzes that new order and its effects with a thoroughness perhaps never surpassed in all the works to follow. It is in many respects Anderson's closest treatment of the discipline of the machine as that discipline works its way into the souls of the servants of industry.

Hugh McVey, the central figure of the novel, is in a way not a typical product of industrialism. The discipline by which his mind is subdued into a form suitable for technological laborings is partially self-imposed, and because of this he attains in the work a certain stature that would be above the reach of a factory hand who is no more than the passive victim of machine discipline. In addition, McVey is an inventor, an artist, for whom training in industrial modes of thought results in a new kind of creativity.

Anderson's hero begins as the child of a slothful and stagnant Missouri town, possessing little of the native sweetness that Anderson elsewhere detected in the small American community; and McVey's own mind exists in a

7. *Ibid.*, p. 12.

torpor of indistinct dreams. Taking to himself an ideal more dynamic, he forces his body into movement, even of the most pointless kind; he applies his intellect to mathematical problems, in order to overcome its meandering dream, and from there he goes on to the study of mechanics, still as part of a program of self-mastery, a program that in time succeeds. He moves to Ohio and achieves success as an inventor.

Up to this point, evidently, the discipline by which McVey transforms himself into an industrial man has demonstrated an element of worth; it has raised him above his environment, at any rate, and it has entered a working partnership with his imagination, which comes to find in mechanics a more vivid expression. "His inclination to dreams, balked by the persistent holding of his mind to definite things, began to reassert itself in a new form, and his brain played no more with pictures of clouds and men in agitated movement but took hold of steel, wood, and iron. Dumb masses of materials taken out of the earth and the forests were molded by his mind into fantastic shapes"; his dreams "that he had fought, had by the strength of his persistency twisted into new channels so that they had expressed themselves in definite things. . . ."[8] Machine technology has proved itself a mold in which raw intuitive materials might be pressed into expressive form.

Yet despite the benefits that a training in technology brings to the hero in giving structure to his imagination, the effect of the training is to imprison whatever imaginative impulses do not bear directly upon mechanical invention. McVey succeeds in smothering not only a wandering habit of mind but instinct and spontaneity as well. Much of the novel is occupied with a married life in which,

8. *Poor White* (New York: B. W. Huebsch, 1920), pp. 70, 252.

on McVey's part, attention has been settled so rigidly upon technological matters, desire has been so clogged and suppressed, that much time is to pass before the final barriers between husband and wife are broken down.

The sexual question upon which *Poor White* touches would become more important in Anderson's later work. Two subsequent novels, *Many Marriages* (1923) and *Dark Laughter* (1925), probe more broadly the problems of sexual constraint and expression. But Anderson was to return to the machine, his interest centered now upon the factory itself, and upon machinery in its actual form and workings.

In a letter of March 11, 1930, Anderson told of his feeling, for the previous four or five years, "that the most interesting thing going on in American life is inside the factories," and of his desire "to get the beauty and poetry of the machine, but at the same time its significance to labor."[9] As reflected in a description, published in 1929, of mill labor in Elizabethton, Tennessee,[10] Anderson was by this time turning toward both elements in the problem of the machine; and in works that followed, he explored the factory in depth—its beauty and its pressures upon its tenders.

At its simplest, Anderson demonstrated, the pressure is upon human nerve. Describing an automobile plant in *Perhaps Women*, Anderson pictured the fineness of calculation with which management strove to speed up the work to the limit to which the nerve of the workers could

9. *Letters of Sherwood Anderson,* selected and edited with an introduction and notes by Howard Mumford Jones in association with Walter B. Rideout (Boston: Little, Brown and Company, 1953), pp. 210–211.

10. In *Nearer the Grass Roots, by Sherwood Anderson, and by the same author, an account of a journey—Elizabethton* (San Francisco: The Westgate Press, 1929).

adjust. Eight hours a day in such a factory, he proposed, might be longer than twelve or sixteen in the old, less disciplined plants. There was no laughter, none of the playful interruptions that broke into the work routine of the earlier factories. "It is all a matter of calculation. You feel it when you go in. You feel rigid lines. You feel movement. You feel a strange tension in the air. There is a quiet terrible intensity."[11]

Exhaustion of nerves was, in Anderson's view of the machine, one of the most direct effects of the factory upon men, but it was perhaps the least subtle. He feared the coming of an impotence, a draining of the strength, will, and pride of men. The idea attains its fullness in *Perhaps Women*.

In that work, as will be seen, Anderson did laud the beauty and power of the machine. The point was, however, even in a way fundamental to his criticism of industrialism. For it is precisely in possessing the qualities of strength, grace, and accuracy, he believed, that the machines crush the men who tend them.

They do so, first, by robbing men of the opportunity to express themselves in craft. The place of craftsmanship in life was, of course, a major preoccupation for Anderson. In *Poor White*, he had dramatized in the person of the harnessmaker Joe Wainsworth the defeat of the craftsman in a machine society; in *A Story Teller's Story*, in *Dark Laughter*, in *Sherwood Anderson's Notebook* (1926) he had discussed the meaning of craft to the man who exercises it. And *A Story Teller's Story* warns that a man is made impotent when he is robbed of work that is skilled and expressive. "His maleness slips imperceptibly from him and he can no longer give himself in love, either to

11. *Perhaps Women* (New York: Liveright, 1931), pp. 18–29.

work or to women."[12] In *Perhaps Women*, the theme of impotence and the decline of craft reappears.[13] But machines do more than abolish craftsmanship. They destroy manhood by their very power and efficiency, before which the one who tends them is made to feel inferior; while a man who derives from a machine a sense of a power that he thinks to be his own cheats himself and deserts his maleness. The harm, however, is to men alone, not women. Woman possesses a "hidden inner life" that is beyond the reach of the machine, and through her immunity she may be the force that will in time overpower machinery.[14]

Yet if machinery, in its power and its intricate perfection, is a menace to its laborers, it is also in the keeping of a class of men in whom its discipline is a condition of health, of artistic and craftsmanlike self-expression, rather than of the atrophy of artistic selfhood. Anderson had demonstrated the idea when in *Poor White* he told of the struggle and fusion of imagination and discipline within the spirit of Hugh McVey. In his later writing, with its emphasis upon the beauty and exquisite play of the machine, the author again paid his respects to the technician, the poet of the machine, and to his disciplined intellect.

In these works, Anderson did not, as in *Poor White*, communicate the sense of opposites in contention and synthesis. Technological invention and supervision becomes simply a coldly beautiful poetic endeavor—which Anderson might admire while not entirely accepting it. But always in the poets of industry, as he pictured them, there is an almost chilling constraint—a clean and narrow, if passionate, attentiveness toward technology that seems more an exclusion of emotion than an expressiveness of art,

12. *A Story Teller's Story*, p. 195.
13. *Perhaps Women*, pp. 41–42, 44.
14. *Ibid.*, pp. 46, 48, 104–107, 140.

yet one that blends at the same time into the act of poetic technological creation, imparting to the act an icy purity.

In the novel *Beyond Desire*—where, despite his harsh portrayal of the condition of factory workers, Anderson referred to,the technological sense as "America at its best, at its finest"—America's industrial mind, in its intensity, is symbolized in the figure of a mill superintendent. The man is given few appealing traits; nothing in him responds to human life inside the factory, or to anything outside. Yet beneath the frosted surface of the superintendent lives an impassioned sensitivity to machines that is the counterpart to his indifference toward the rest of existence, and in his grasp of the machine and attention to it there is a sure strength and an unboasting integrity.[15]

An even greater emphasis upon the frigid tensity of technological thinking, and upon the artistic in that pattern of thought, is to be found in *Perhaps Women*. It is clear that the young chemists, inventors, aviators, and plant managers in whom dwell the modern spirit have no time for the cultivation of a wide, earthy imagination and experience. "They were clean young men without vices. They studied hard, did things well. . . . They were the figures of the new age, cold men, clear men, impersonal men." Still, the lyricism in their nature does reveal itself, in a form more detached and crisply lined. A young Lindbergh touched with poetry, Anderson styled a certain mill engineer; and the author described one engineer whose hearing could pick out every small sound that went into the roar of a factory room. "He had an ear developed like the ear of a fine musician and in another age might have been a musician."[16] If, in *Perhaps Women* and *Beyond Desire* as against *Poor White*, machine art is not broken down into components of

15. *Beyond Desire* (New York: Liveright, 1932), pp. 26–27, 50–51.
16. *Perhaps Women*, pp. 45–46, 68–69, 101, 109–110, 124.

discipline and intuition—if, in truth, the inventor or technician appears to possess for machinery a serene attachment for which no continual act of will and discipline would be the necessary basis—he is nonetheless as tightly, as obsessively narrowed in his experience of life as Hugh McVey, and as rhapsodic in his obsession.

### The Machine as Aesthetic

In *Poor White*, an image for the emerging American industrial complex is that of a giant. The giant has little of loveliness, and its dominance spells desolation for all that was lovely before its advent, but even in its destructiveness it possesses its own majesty.

As the monster marched across the land, "great coal fields from which was to be taken food to warm the blood in the body of the giant were being opened up"; again, "the roar and clatter of the breathing of the terrible new thing, half hideous, half beautiful in its possibilities," could be heard throughout the nation. The dumping mechanism invented by Hugh McVey

> made a new kind of poetry in railroad yards and along rivers at the back of cities where ships are loaded. On city nights as you lie in your houses you may hear suddenly a long reverberating roar. It is a giant that has cleared his throat of a carload of coal.

The new factory that comes to the Ohio town of Bidwell through McVey's mechanical genius seems to his future wife "not a factory but a powerful animal, a powerful beast-like thing that Hugh had tamed and made useful to his fellows."[17]

Here the machine has achieved a massive stature in counterpoise to its emotional repressions. In *Puzzled*

17. *Poor White*, pp. 62–63, 231, 253.

*America,* the machine again appears in its mass and grandeur.

Written during the depression and social upheaval of the thirties, *Puzzled America* represents both a new departure and a culmination of concerns developed in the course of Anderson's career. As is much of his work, it is an exploration into the American character; and it resembles *Perhaps Women* and the essay on Elizabethton in being not a novel but a set of impressions personally gained, an observation of people and things en masse. But the range of *Puzzled America* is greater, its subject and treatment more diffuse, than are the range and subject of *Perhaps Women*; it passes over the extent of the country, from region to region, class to class, and works toward an interpretation of a whole depression-wracked people. And it is a far more affirmative book than are many of the author's earlier writings; for it seeks an answer to the challenge to America thrown down by the depression and discovers the answer in the strength of the American land and the democratic strength of the people.

At one point in the work, therefore, the machines of the Tennessee Valley Authority are seen to represent gigantically creative force. Anderson wrote of the Wilson Dam:

> There is a song, the song of the great motors. You are stirred. Something in you—the mechanically-minded American in you, begins to sing. Everything is so huge, so suggestive of power and at the same time so delicate. You walk about muttering.
>
> "No wonder the Russians wanted our engineers," you say to yourself.
>
> The great motors sing on, each motor as large as a city room. There is a proud kind of rebirth of Americanism in you.
>
> "Some of our boys did this," you say to yourself, throwing out your chest.

Nor are the machines separate from the strong land; they coalesce with it to form a single organism powerful of sinew. In *Puzzled America*, Anderson made little distinction between the soil of the continent and America's richness in other kinds. He conceived of water power as a new form of wealth in the land, and of the Tennessee Valley Authority he exulted: "Power stored to make a steady stream of power—power from the Wilson being used to build the Joe Wheeler and the Norris—the river being made to harness itself. There is a new kind of poetry in that thought." Here was power to be used to nourish small industries, to reduce the costs of power in towns, to extend electricity to homes: "the money coming in to go back into the country out of which the power came"; and through the great movement to reclaim and develop the Valley, stripped hills might be reclothed in forests, the bleeding of soil be stanched.[18]

Finally, in a section of Anderson's *Memoirs*, land and industry again come into unity, and industry is once more an expression of energy rather than of repression. Anderson detected in Chicago the "beauty of the loose and undisciplined, unfinished and unlimited," and he placed the metropolis in a setting of land and industrialism:

> A city to be a real one has to have something back of it. Land, a lot of it. Rich land—corn, wheat, iron, rivers, mountains, hogs, cattle. Chicago back of it has the Middle West—the empire called Mid-America. Corn, hogs, wheat, iron, coal, industrialism—a new age moving across a continent by railroads, moving unbelievable quantities of goods across a vast place, in the center of which Chicago stands.[19]

18. *Puzzled America* (New York and London: Charles Scribner's Sons, 1935), pp. 58–60.

19. *Sherwood Anderson's Memoirs* (New York: Harcourt, Brace and Company, 1942), pp. 108–109.

In such manner, Anderson delineated the machine in its more energetic character. But some of Anderson's writing in praise of the beauty of machinery had to do with poetic qualities more subdued. His increasing ambition, by the end of the postwar decade, to grasp the beauty of machinery reflected, as we have seen, a fascinated conception of the delicate complexity and precision of the modern factory:

> There, in that machine, what seemed at first disorder in movement becoming a vast, a beautiful order.
>
> Why, a man goes a little daft.
>
> A thousand, perhaps in the life of such a machine a hundred million, white balls, each containing to the hundredth part of an inch, the same yardage of slender thread . . .
>
> They dancing down steel hallways, every hop, every skip calculated, they landing at little steel doors, never missing . . .
>
> They being touched, handled, directed by fingers of steel.
>
> Never harshly to break thread that I could break easily between my two fingers.[20]

The Tennessee Valley system impressed Anderson in its delicacy as well as its might: indeed, its power is not the power in tumult of Chicago, but power in order, directed toward determined ends.[21] In the exact and graceful form of the machine, poetry and discipline touch: the cool and ordered poetry of technology, sensitive to detail and relation, that is the discipline of the machine technician.

20. *Perhaps Women*, p. 122.
21. *Puzzled America*, p. 59. Also see Anderson's description of the factory and its machinery—"a play of light and colors in a great clean space"—in "The Times and the Towns," an essay in *America as Americans See It*, edited by Fred J. Ringel (New York: Harcourt, Brace and Company, 1932), p. 16.

# Chapter 3

# Waldo Frank THE MACHINE
## IN CULTURAL FERMENT

T HE writings of Waldo Frank represent twentieth-century American literature at its most experimental —eager in artistic innovation and in the assimilation of the modern intellect. Set beside the work of Anderson, that of Frank suggests the contrast of Anderson's Mid-America to the upper middle-class Manhattan of Frank's childhood— the provincial to the cosmopolitan, the native American idiom to the stark intellectual formulation. But in no way has it been Frank's intention to develop a body of thought that would stand apart from the American environment. Few writers have in fact striven so persistently for the ideal of cultural wholeness: for the fusion of the parts of the American soul—and beyond, the soul of the modern world—as Catholicism unified the parts of medieval Europe.

Men and cultures, Frank has argued, may exist in one of two states: wholeness or disintegration. A man is whole when the "cosmic dimension" in him—that dimension of his spirit that encounters and senses God as Being and Whole, underlying and bringing unity to the multiplicity of things—is dominant over his ego dimension and all his faculties, and, living his participation in Being, he possesses unity within himself, with his fellows, and with the totality of existence. A society is whole when its members are whole and in harmony with each other—when society enacts its participation in Being and its work and institutions and creations sing of Being. Disintegration, for man or culture, amounts to a loss of the sense of God, hence a loss of unity both within and without the self; it entails the domination of will over love and therefore the dissolution of self and society into fragmented, unrelated impulses of will. Such, in Frank's interpretation, is the condition of modern Western civilization. Yet, while identifying the disintegration as a sign of cultural failure, he also saw its chaotic profusion of energetic materials as potentially the basis for a future rebirth of culture, the emergence of a new unity vital in its blending of vital fragments.

Since the disintegration of culture in the modern era forms the theme of Frank's writing, the machine—or rather, the machine as it is shaped and employed by the modern will—must appear as a fact of disintegration. Here Frank's portrayal of industrialism attains a similarity, at least aesthetic and imaginative, to the portrayal by other writers of the machine in its bulk and energy. Frank recognized an industrial discipline as well. But the discipline is itself in large measure a product of disintegration, when the machine, as the instrument of the fragmented will, turns upon its master, captures the will and subdues it to the terms and processes of the machine. And this reversal is made possible only because modern man is in possession of no cultural Whole within which the will might see and pursue its true ends, and machinery might be tamed and harnessed to true human service. Chaos and regimentation are seen by Frank not as separate characteristics of the machine age but as a single situation, and it is for purposes of analysis that we here examine them separately.

## The Disintegration of the West

Frank's most definite statement of a philosophy of history, upon which in considerable measure he based his interpretation of the machine, is to be found in three works —*The Re-discovery of America, Chart for Rough Water*, and *The Rediscovery of Man*—which reflected his thinking as of the late twenties, the early days of the Second World War, and the mid-fifties. *Our America*, published a decade before *The Re-discovery of America*, hints of the historical view elaborated in the later works of social criticism. And at the foundation of that view is Frank's mystical perception of life—a perception that suffuses his novels and stories.

The characters typically appear in varying states of unity or disunity with life; and, consciously or unconsciously, directly or with hesitation and with fatal blunder, they seek unity. Their spiritual progress seems always to be marked in flashes of intuition in which they perceive their oneness with Being, flashes of self-giving love through which they are made one with other human flesh and spirit; their retrogression, in destructive acts or in sproutings of sterile, self-centered, or incomplete love. The themes that are the tissue of Frank's novels receive more direct exposition in his social and historical works and provide a foundation for historical interpretation.

In those works, he insisted that society becomes sound

in achieving a unity of parts and reflecting the greater wholeness of existence; and he maintained that these had been the triumphs of Europe's Christian culture, especially in its development of what, in *Chart for Rough Water*, Frank called the "Great Tradition." By the phrase he meant the Western concept of the person, a concept in which individual personality is affirmed in the very fact of recognition that personality is grounded in Oneness. The Great Tradition *"is the knowledge that individual man partakes of the divine, which is his way of naming the universal and of naming it good and of naming it his. It is the knowledge that his life has purpose and direction because God is in him."*[1]

The Great Tradition is therefore no denial of the person, no attainment of oneness through the negation of multiplicity. It is a simultaneous and harmonious exaltation of the person, who is substanced and projected out of ultimate Whole, ultimate Being; and of the Whole, acting and manifested in persons. And this exaltation of the person, which is the strength of Western culture, is also the agent that, misdirected, led to the decline of cultural unity. European culture splintered when atomistic self-assertion replaced the service of God as the ideal of human behavior, and the transformation was effected when the *"individual soul, fed and grown great by its awareness of the divine within it, believed it could dispense with the divine."*[2] In so believing, the soul proceeded into chaos.

In his release from cultural order, Frank insisted, man returned to a state of savagery. Self became his universe, and the "impulse of the fragmentary man—the will for

1. *Chart for Rough Water: Our Role in a New World* (New York: Doubleday, Doran and Company, 1940), p. 50. Italics here and throughout the chapter are Frank's.
2. *Ibid.*, p. 51.

personal aggrandisement"—"exteriorised itself from the whole of human life," and pushed aside every other impulse. Finally, it became *"literally* embodied" in the machine. In the end, the man who has exalted will, and who has substituted, for love, power that is the instrument of will, has been made servile and passive. He is servile because he has yielded to power in himself, and, in accepting its primacy, has no defense against any hostile power that may attempt to dominate him. He is passive because power operates externally to man—unlike love, which merges the world with the self. Power moves on by its own momentum, dragging after it the self that hungers for ever more power; it materializes in the form of the machine, which performs labors for man in such fashion as to exclude his positive participation and thereby renders him the passive recipient of goods he cannot meaningfully assimilate.[3]

In such manner, Frank described the illness of a society that has ruptured into fragments. But he saw more than illness. Where the cultural fragments are rich and forceful in their self-will, he detected the basis for the creation of a vital new Whole.

We have seen that when Frank talked of social and spiritual unity, he did not envision a monolith. He conceived of a culture possessing a harmony of lushly diverse parts. The Great Tradition amounted to no suppression of the self, but to its enrichment—an enrichment so great that personality became puffed up with its own magnificence and forgot the foundations of its strength. The author maintained that for both individuals and races the stage of power must precede the stage of love.

3. *The Re-discovery of America: An Introduction to a Philosophy of American Life* (New York and London: Charles Scribner's Sons, 1929), pp. 77–78, 83–87.

[B]y means of Power [the human] spirit is cultivated and developed. Only the ego which is strong, self-assertive, prone to Power, is ripe for Love. Love is no submergence of a weak personal will in others: it is the masterful, conscious fusion of the strong ego with life.

It is because of this that Christianity has made so much of the strong sinner who repents.[4] And chaos, when—as in America—it is a stirring of energetic cultural particles, is a promising beginning, both because its variety gives hope of a complex cultural order and because its energy, if redirected, may be an impelling toward unity.

### Disintegration and the Machine

The American city, Frank showed in *Our America*, is a vibrant and imposing thing—vibrant in the force it has drained from its ensnared, driven, depleted citizens. "Its high white towers are arrows of will: its streets are the plowings of passionate desire," he described New York; a "lofty, arrogant, lustful city, beaten through by an iron rhythm." And again he said of our metropolitan giants: "These clamorous buildings drip energy. This iron world is a tissue of complex human wills." True, he went on to describe this "delirium of stone," which has cowed and subdued its own creators, as "but a scum on the energies of men," who might instead draw from themselves higher creative powers.[5] But still the passage represents one of Frank's earlier depictions of America's urban and industrial complex as throbbing, and implicitly anarchic, energy.

As the author further developed his cultural and social criticism of the United States, he drew sharper focus upon the anarchy that underlies American civilization and upon the relationship between anarchy and the machine. Hence-

4. *Ibid.*, p. 80.
5. *Our America* (New York: Boni and Liveright, 1919), pp. 171, 221.

forth, the accent would be not upon industrial energy itself, but upon the industrial chaos that in the literature
of the period is revealed in aesthetic kinship to the energy
of the world of pulsant steel.

An essay of the mid-twenties indicates Frank's general
conception of the chaotic American environment. In this
piece he was objecting to the attempt by *avant-garde*
writers to incorporate Dada into American literature; his
grounds were that "America *is* Dada," and that what was
needed, therefore, was a counter-tendency in American
writing.

> Dada spans Brooklyn Bridge; it spins round Columbus
> Circle; it struts with the Ku-Klux Klan; it mixes with all
> brands of bootleg whiskey; it prances in our shows; it
> preaches in our churches; it tremolos at our political conven-
> tions. . . . It is in the medley of strutting chimneys and bowed
> heads, of strutting precepts and low deeds that make America.

Within this environment, the smart, shocking young author
represented no true departure. Our surface already "twists
and scintillates and shrieks." It was through order and
seriousness that native letters might contribute to the
building of an American culture.[6]

As a symbol of his disordered land, Frank came to employ the image of the jungle; and into the symbolism of
the jungle he worked the machine, along with the other
creatures of the steaming American wilderness. In place
of tarantulas, he said, America possesses machines; "the
intricate pull and stress of economic forces" is our equiv-
alent of the storms and insects and bacteria of nature;
our debris of European culture resembles the ancient cities
to be found in other climes, crumbled into tropic earth,

---

6. *In the American Jungle* (New York and Toronto: Farrar and Rinehart, 1937), pp. 129–131.

Frank said in *The Re-discovery of America.* "We, too, live beneath the whelm of what is *our* external nature; live on the defensive; live submissively beneath the play of forces alien to what we recognise as human and creative." And like their primitive brethren, the American savages worship the most imposing forms discovered in their wilderness.[7]

"The American jungle is rich in denatured elements of a transplanted world. . . ." The values, the morals, the arts to which Americans profess had once been living segments of the European Whole. In a time and place where that culture does not exist, its values can be no more than "rotted tissue," a compost accentuating the jungle-like nature of the environment. But in one respect, Frank indicated, the analogy cannot hold. The Amazon forest, the cultural rot beneath Yucatan, are passive, do not act upon the savages who tread them. In the aggressive jungle of the United States, "We literally are *the hunted*," pursued by the insistent things of our civilization. The reason, essentially, is that *"this world of ours is the exteriorisation of our own desire"*—the will of modern man projected outward and made material in the machine—a jungle so much a part of ourselves that we must adore and cannot escape it.[8]

The machine, therefore, is in Frank's conception the outstanding feature of the American jungle, and so, in one sense, the foremost symbol of America's chaos. Industrialism, he found in another context, is the expression of "organized anarchy."[9] Even on the most superficial level, the machine as it is encountered by men "is not far in kind from the tumid monsters that clutter any jungle." As is nature, the machine is external to man, confronts him from every direction, and demands his painstaking adjustment

7. *The Re-discovery of America*, p. 71.
8. *Ibid.*, pp. 74, 76–78.
9. *Our America*, p. 9.

so that it will sustain his life. "Nature for the American is this iron chaos of life-providing, death-dealing, value-distilling forces."[10]

But most deeply and most chaotically, the machine is for America what it is for the modern world in general: anarchic will made concrete. "The machine is action, particularised and dissociated into a body"; it is the instrument and expression of pure personal will, or rather, some particular part of a will, some particular desire or aim; and our world of machines is a chaos of separate shreds of will.[11] It is true that Frank placed the ultimate blame not upon the machine but upon modern man, who has not found wholeness and so cannot integrate the machine within it—and the author believed that the machine is adaptable to a spiritual order; but within our era machinery, as the most dramatic implement and sign of the atomized will, must be the implement and emblem of anarchy.

In one of its phases, then, our machine-charged chaos is described in the work of Frank as a descent from culture into savagery. But savagery stands at the beginning as well as at the end of a civilization, and Frank also saw our chaotic environment as the rich and varied soil from which could grow the new culture of wholeness.

In *Our America*, the author showed a certain feeling for the vital, formless character of his country. He warned against any attempt to define closely the nature of America.

For only in ignorance of a world so vast and so unformed can certainty survive. America is yet in the inchoate state where it has subjective meaning only. America is a complex of myriad lights playing upon myriad planes. As a Unit it exists only in the eyes of the beholder. Its reality is but a sprawling continent—mountains and gardenland and desert—swarmed

10. *The Re-discovery of America*, pp. 71–72.
11. *Ibid.*, pp. 39–41.

by a sprawling congeries of people. To bound it is to stifle it, to give it a definite character is to emasculate it, to offer it a specific voice is to strike it dumb.[12]

The promise of America lies in the nation's vulgarity, Frank said in an essay of the nineteen twenties. He argued that if we were spiritually faulty and nothing else, we would not be vulgar. We are coarse precisely in the assertiveness with which we display our faults; and that assertiveness is proof of a longing and an effort to attain the peaks.

> High energy we have—energy of the kind known as religious. It vaporizes for lack of a container; or it is misapplied in the pushing of old creeds no longer fit to house it. Emptiness grows emphatic because it strives to be full.

Our madness finds "symbols in motors, dramas in football games, art in advertisements, morality in statutes, and sermons in tabloid papers"; better directed, it could become "supremely sane." "Deflect this misplaced will to unity into some channel that will hold it; and we shall see how the energy which mothers American vulgarity and American folly can father greatness."[13]

In the *Re-discovery of America*, Frank made a similar case. "The dissolution of the Mediterranean Whole lives in us, not as mere decay, but as *ferment*." It is this ferment that impels the American soul to pretenses of beauty and truth; but in our urge is the nation's hope. And in the same work, Frank affirmed the luxuriance of the American jungle. "Our chaos is a variety, wondrously rich, of needs, potentials, natures, values"; the aim should be to "*symphonise*" it, so that order may be attained yet the variety preserved.[14]

12. *Our America*, p. 8.
13. *In the American Jungle*, pp. 109–112. From an article of 1926.
14. *The Re-discovery of America*, pp. 91–92, 205.

Finally, there is one potentially health-giving element in the American chaos, Frank revealed, that is more peculiarly native to us than either the machine or the cultural ferment that is our inheritance from a dissolved medieval civilization. This element is an anarchic energy to be found in the American soil and continent, generated by the hugeness, the contrast, and the violence of the natural environment. "America is a feverish world. Its geological tempo is not like that of Europe. It is far more terribly intense," and the intensity is reflected in a wildness that is one part of the American soul.[15] The vigor of the continent is conjoined to that of American society: Frank spoke of "the enormous energy of the American world, made manifest in our tumultuous mountains, in our sea-like plains, in our meteor climates, in our cities, in our babel of folks."[16] The American land, spacious and potent, was for Frank as for Anderson a permanent leavening to the American spirit.

And just as Frank discovered within the total American ferment the substances for the building of a new culture—and the energy with which to heat and empower the act of construction—so also did he find the machine a material to be worked into the cultural Whole. In *The Re-discovery of America,* he insisted that the

> present capacity of the machine to surround man, to determine the forms and colours of his acts, to hold his energy and his allegiance, is a negative reflex of man's incapacity as yet to create a Whole in modern terms, and to assimilate the machine as a means and a symbol within it.[17]

And in "The Machine and Metaphysics" (1925), Frank looked toward a healthy integration of machinery into the

15. *In the American Jungle*, pp. 126–127. From an essay of 1925.
16. *The Re-discovery of America*, p. 141.
17. *Ibid.*, p. 42.

human soul, as the soul has already mastered and incorporated the tool. The apparently unresolvable differences between tool and machine, he acknowledged. The tool is the passive implement of the craftsman, possesses no power outside his own, responds utterly and immediately to his will, and so becomes an extension of himself and a means to his self-expression; the machine pursues its own pace and method and seemingly excludes the participation of the attendant. But the difficulty, Frank contended, lies ultimately in the human consciousness.

Unquestionably, he believed, there was a time when primitive man had not yet achieved the psychological adjustment that would enable him to recognize as an element of his own will the piece of stone or wood, the dugout or the horse that he employed. We stand just as primitive before the machine. And when we have made the leap of consciousness, we will have won a triumph greater than that over the tool. For the tool is a part of external nature, and in mastering it we master only a portion of external existence; the machine is already a function of human will, and in our conquest of it, we "shall have won a victory of consciousness not merely over the nature of the external world —but over our own nature."[18]

### Discipline and the Machine

In a passage in *America Hispana*, Frank pictured the Panama Canal as an embodiment of a technology clean-formed and disciplined, symbolic of the United States.

> The Zone is a swath of utter aloofness, cut through the planturous height of Panamá. . . . The Culebra Cut is a gash in the mountain's face. Jagged and wild with verdure, its two lips rise against the fastidious Canal and against the vessels neatly puffing through the continent. . . .

18. *In the American Jungle*, pp. 153–157.

. . . . Long masses of cement, high hinges of steel, become a being of will: a creature nervous and tense-purposed like a hand. Its gray sobriety is apart from the luxuriance of nature. Its wilfulness is victor over a voluptuary world that will lift no vessels, that would bar all vessels. Silent, invisibly moved, star-aloof, star-precise, the hand of man grasps the boat in its concrete fingers, raises it, pushes it along to the next hand, which lifts it farther. . . .

Rails and a road border the Canal and serve its precision. . . . The flag of the United States snaps in the trade wind from its concrete towers. The flag transforms the tropic air, making it cool. It waves back Panamá, making it alien.[19]

As a thing of fine tension in balanced, precisioned composure, the Canal has its stature; yet Frank believed that as an instrument of policy on the part of the United States, the Canal remained foreign to the land through which it sliced, while its purpose should be to unite in spirit the Americas.

Frank's description of the Panama Canal pays its respects—in a manner, through elegance of language and poetry of image, at any rate—to the rigorous purities of machine technology, even while criticizing the uses to which the Canal is put. And how dramatic the contrasts, when the passage is set beside others from the body of Frank's writings; how abruptly the polarity within American culture confronts the reader! In the Canal, the crazy flux of Dada America settles into poise and form; the scorching jungle, prowled by iron beasts, its topography broken by mountainous skyscrapers eruptive of a volcanic energy, transforms itself into a landscape Northern, silent, and stern. Elsewhere in his writings, Frank portrayed the machine and its disciplines in contours less sharp and less

19. *America Hispana: A Portrait and a Prospect* (New York and London: Charles Scribner's Sons, 1931), pp. 16–17.

chaste than those he detected and traced within the Canal —but in contours and colorings that imply nonetheless the dominion of the machine over mind and body.

In essence, of course, even the regimentation imposed by the machine is in Frank's understanding largely a product of cultural disintegration. It is the outcome of a state of affairs in which the will, lacking the direction that only a culture of wholeness can provide, becomes the slave of its own desires and its own iron creations, and in which the machine, lacking a cultural Whole into which it could be fixed, flies out of control and bears with it the fractured will that had hoped to be its master. But in *Our America*, Frank contributed a still further elaboration to his analysis of industrialism; he suggested its close relationship both to the American frontier and to the "Puritanism" about which writers of the postwar decade had so much to say.

Puritanism would seem to have been an ally to the frontier. The pioneer adopted a system of moral repression, argued the author of *Our America*—in a passage that does not refer directly to Puritanism itself—because in order to perform his urgent tasks he needed a technique of self-mastery—a technique of denial that would close off every outlet for human energy save one, and would direct into the channel of material effort such dammed-up reserves of force that the threatening wilderness could be conquered before the wilderness destroyed the pioneer. And this self-mastery would have the effect of a harsh asceticism. For the pioneer was a civilized man and could not exist naturally and comfortably within the wilds, as primitive man had learned to do. "The pioneer must do violence upon himself. Whole departments of his psychic life must be repressed. Categories of desire must be inhibited. Reaches of consciousness must be lopped off." He must reawaken in himself ancient intuitions. "Virtues which lent themselves to material conquest and to endurance were extolled: virtues which called for inner peace or levied energy without a manifest material return were vices." The pioneer must ignore his own inner experience; and he rejected "that vicarious experience which is art."[20]

The pioneer inhibitions were balanced by "the inviting immensities of the American field," which encouraged exterior activity. "The pioneer became a man, innerly locked up, outwardly released."[21] Energy flowed into the job of subduing the wilderness, and that work merged inseparably with the accumulation of wealth. And by its own momentum, the pioneer spirit carried itself beyond the period in which it was needed.

Finally, the pioneer impulse fixed itself in one of its own productions, where it might live beyond its time; it helped bring about the machine, which then reproduced on its own the frontier rhythm of existence. (American industrialism, Frank said at another point, is "the new Puritanism.") The machine is the natural embodiment of energies turned outward. "Energy poured to the surfaces of life. The machine is simply an appendage to the human body. The normally balanced man had hands and feet of flesh. The extraverted man had hands and feet of iron." But the machine is more than a creature of human forces.

> For if the machine is the fresh product of the outpouring human soul, it soon became its master, and the soul that made it could not cease to feed it. Thus the new external world— the industrial world which America had created now drove

20. *Our America*, pp. 18–21. In another passage, Frank explicitly identified this relationship between Puritanism and the frontier. *Ibid.*, p. 63.

21. *Ibid.*, p. 20.

the American out into an endless exteriorization. A sucking monster, which as it sucked swelled larger and so sucked more. Feed the machine of life. Do not stop. Open your veins![22]

In his descriptions of the energetic American city, Frank employed exactly this notion of the servitude of the people to their metallic world, the draining of their vitality into the steel and concrete masses that surround them.[23] For *Our America*, therefore, there is a kind of indirect juxtaposition and a form of reconciliation between the two concepts of industrial discipline and industrial energy.

Yet while Frank assaulted much of the regimentation of Puritan moralism and of the machine, he granted both a place in the ordering of human existence. His understanding of the machine as a positive force in the better disposing of society had to do with the *surface* organization that machinery might bring to civilization, rather than with the disciplining of mind and impulse itself. Within a certain complex of American characteristics of which Puritanism is an element, on the other hand, Frank at one point detected a discipline that might—within one peculiar set of circumstances, and one only—undergo a transfiguration and work its way *inward* to the benefit of the American soul.

In *The Re-discovery of America*, Frank applauded the machine for its work in binding into a single entity the continental land of the United States. By the use of the machine, we are able "to realise for our nation an imaginative, plastic, communicable form"; to give us what is for every people a healthy possession—"a land in which it can behold the focus and the symbol of its creative impulse."

22. *Ibid.*, pp. 44–45, 98.
23. *Ibid.*, pp. 171, 221. Also see p. 40, above.

In 1865, the sparse-settled empire [of the United States] was held, against the pull of its sections, by the machine. Not Lincoln's armies, so much as the telegraph, the railroad, the new will of industrial expansion saved our continental nation. The machine replaced for us the communicable bond, in . . . . earlier vast lands, of church or monarch

it has made the country "plastically real—an accessible physical experience for the people."[24]

In *Dawn in Russia*, Frank assigned much the same role to the machine in Russian history—the role of bringing structure and order, less to the human mind and human nerve itself in any direct way than to the exterior of society, building a social framework within which can develop a culture that nourishes the spirit. Before the machine, he said, Russia was vital, but her vitality was not ordered and was therefore not strength. It was the order of industry that brought the peasants to the towns, made of them an activist body of workers, coalesced and wrought into strength Russia's dispersed vitalities. Machinery, "binding every part of a people with every other part, fulfills its social body," provides a surface structure.

> Russia, even more than old pioneer America, needs surface: the delimiting factor that brings organic life to a human mass lost in a continent. More even than new America, it worships the machine which promises to give it surface. . . .[25]

This fruitful ordering would however be only of the surface of civilization, and when in Frank's portrait of the Panama Canal he dealt with an ordered technology apparently mated internally to the soul of the United States— as technological discipline was wedded to the souls of

24. *The Re-discovery of America*, pp. 232–233.
25. *Dawn in Russia: The Record of a Journey* (New York and London: Charles Scribner's Sons, 1932), pp. 72–74, 209.

Anderson's inventors and engineers—Frank was offering no extravagant praise. When at one juncture Frank discussed America's Puritan moralism, in association with a few related American traits, as a potentially healthy discipline, he conceived of a discipline merged with the American spirit in its deepest recesses.

In only a single connection did Frank acknowledge in that moralism a positive and permanent value—its agency in the subduing of the raw and elemental American continent. On more than one occasion Frank identified, in the different human civilizations that had come into contact with the continent, evidences of a spontaneous rebound away from its violence and toward order. "The Indian," he said in *Our America*, "met the strain of his world with a passionate restraint. Reserve became so deep a portion of his life that it can be no less than the need of life which caused it."[26] In another instance, and speaking of the whole continent, South America as well as North, Frank spotted a relationship between constraint and the land's energy so close that it is one almost of similarity rather than of reaction: "This energy tends towards a passional restraint. . . ."[27]

Frank developed his ideas most fully in an essay of 1925, where he bolstered his thesis by reference to the findings of Carl Jung, who had discovered in Americans he had psychoanalyzed "a unique alliance of *wildness and restraint* which did not exist in the European nature." Taking the straightness of American streets as the symbol of our restraint—for the curve is intrinsic to nature and the mind, while the straight line and the angle jarringly resist nature—the author found that a similar restraint had helped in the eventual formation of an American Indian culture within the flaming continent. "I am certain that when the

26. *Our America*, p. 5.
27. *The Re-discovery of America*, p. 229.

ancestors of the Indian crossed to America from Mongolia (or Atlantis) they resisted this atmospheric fury, as have we, with an angular restraint." But that was only the first stage; a whole culture must come with the reconciliation of the opposing forces.

> The Indian culture began when his innate spiritual and intellectual values formed a solution with the world about him: his culture was achieved when the responses between his soul and the world had rounded into a unified *life* which expressed both fully. After many ages, the Indian's first reactive restraint toned down, and became the subtle and fertile curve of the Indian music, the symbolic gesture of his dance, the exquisite reticence of his demeanor.

And in like manner, in phenomena so diverse as our Puritans and morals, our dress and our straight streets, "we manifest the first stage of resistance to the furious fire which is the nature of our world. The rigid angles will smooth out, will take on the curves of life—will become the forms of our American culture."[28]

28. *In the American Jungle*, pp. 123–127.

# Chapter 4

# John Dos Passos

## THE LIBERTARIAN CAUSE

JOHN DOS PASSOS is perhaps best known for his persistent dissensions from the predominant political and social moods of the nation. In the years immediately following the First World War, when America was congratulating itself upon the success of its spectacular wartime adventure, Dos Passos was among the young writers, fresh from the campaigns, who attempted to reveal the horror and absurdity of the thing in which they had participated. More deeply, his early works are an expression of the aesthetic revolt, common to his literary generation, from America's machine culture. By the late nineteen twenties, Dos Passos was a vocal, though independent, leftist—and contributor to the *New Masses*—at a time of relative political calm, well before the depression had thrown other

American authors into association with the left. At about the middle of the depression decade, perhaps before the completion of the trilogy *U. S. A.—The 42nd Parallel* (1930), *Nineteen Nineteen* (1932), *The Big Money* (1936) —Dos Passos shifted for a time to the center in American politics and gave his support to the Roosevelt reforms. Thereafter he continued the move toward the right that today makes him, once again, a critic of America's contemporary political tendency.

Dos Passos has been, however, a dissenter of singularly broad temperament. Even in his days of association with the *New Masses*, he was calling for a reformism that would fit the unique conditions of the American nation; and in *The Big Money*, the final novel of *U. S. A.*, he appealed from the corruptions of twentieth-century America to the American tradition of liberty. His present conservatism appears to reflect a sane and genial trust in the less centralized political organisms of the American past and a conviction that the shift of power toward Washington and the unions, however necessary in its beginnings, may become a threat equal to that which it once countered. Dos Passos has always suspected dominant power; yet during most of his career he has been ready to look closest about him, to his native land, for the means and traditions to resist power.

Thus if a single theme can be said to run through the work of Dos Passos, it is the theme of liberty, always opposed by some contemporary tendency in American society. But Dos Passos subjected both freedom and its antithesis to constant redefinition—or, perhaps, to a constantly evolving definition. For the sake of convenience, that evolution may be divided into three periods, in each of which the concepts of freedom and tyranny were given some distinctive accent and artistic formulation. Yet it must be emphasized that this arbitrary[1] schematization refers not so much to the inner development of the thought and vision of Dos Passos, but rather to shifts in the exterior form in which he expressed his vision.

The earliest period covers only a few years after the end of the First World War. The definition of freedom that emerges from the author's writings of those years is of freedom as self-expression in the domain of the aesthetic, the imaginative, the humanely sensuous: in effect, his stories were of the "artist" against society. Also, the fiction was as yet centered upon a small number of individuals and their efforts to salvage freedom within themselves. And consequently, when the machine appears it is treated more directly and closely than in his work of the nineteen thirties and after. The limited number of characters and the relative understatement of specifically political themes gave compactness to the narrative; the concentration upon the single personality—sensitive, isolated, and quite articulate in his spiritual wants—made it possible to establish clearly the values against which worked the disciplines of the machine, or those of its allies.

In two writings of the young Dos Passos, *Three Soldiers* (1921) and the play "The Moon Is a Gong" (1923)—or "The Garbage Man," as it came to be entitled in its publication of 1926—the mating of libertarianism with aestheticism is especially pronounced. Together the novel and the

---

1. The pattern I shall outline differs considerably from that suggested in John H. Wrenn's penetrating *John Dos Passos* (New York: Twayne Publishers, 1962). Many of the important writings of Dos Passos I do not discuss directly; the selection and grouping I employ are of use only to relate the work of Dos Passos to the topics with which I am concerned: technology, mechanical discipline, the greater range and energy of machine society.

play may be taken to represent a particular statement; and nothing produced after 1923 would be quite so explicit in its defense of youth and sensibility and romantic urge.

A marking out of a second stage in the evolution of a social viewpoint on the part of Dos Passos is more difficult, especially because "The Garbage Man" touches upon this as upon his earlier period. No single criterion can be employed by which to join together, or to separate, the works that appeared between the early twenties and the end of the thirties—when the novel *Adventures of a Young Man* signaled a further turn in the writing of Dos Passos. In theme, "The Garbage Man" clearly belongs with the earliest fiction and completes its argument; in its tone of fantasy, the play has something in common with passages from *Manhattan Transfer* (1925), while the two stand distinct both from *Three Soldiers* and from *U. S. A.*; in structure, *Manhattan Transfer* looks ahead, in some measure, to the famous trilogy.

But the play and the novels that followed are all distinguishable from *Three Soldiers* in at least one way: in them the massiveness, the energy of machine civilization itself has assumed major importance. In *Three Soldiers*, the story of the young protagonists and particularly of John Andrews is always at the forefront; in "The Garbage Man," on the other hand, we are equally aware of the lovers and of the thing of restive steel within which they are entangled: it seems to possess a deranged personality of its own. If machine society in "The Garbage Man" is an agitant density of metal, in *Manhattan Transfer* it is a density of humankind, and *U. S. A.* thickens that human density and expands its range. And both *Nineteen Nineteen* and *The Big Money*, the second and final novels of the trilogy, define a libertarian manner of comparable magnitude. No longer fixing itself to the more fragile impulses of the individual spirit, liberty has now become the right of a nation and can assert itself in public events.

The third period that we may distinguish in the development of the author's social critique is roughly coincident, even for our purposes, with his shift to the political center and ultimately to the conservative ranks. At this time, he was giving further refinement to his understanding of American libertarianism. His revolutionary ardor abated, he could now see our instinct for freedom as a cool adherence to constitutional methods, a capacity for compromise and self-restraint. Occasionally he would indicate that this instinct can take form in a raw and forceful thrust toward freedom, such as that which moves the social protestors in the interpolated comment of *The Big Money*; but a sense of the steadiness of our political conduct has come to modify the representation, so that America's political energies appear in fusion with the political disciplines of the Anglo-American tradition.

*First Period: One Man's Initiation, Three Soldiers,*
*"The Garbage Man"*

By 1919 or 1920, and perhaps earlier, Dos Passos had already turned left. The fact must be held in mind as a counterpoise to the more explicit tone and mood to be found in his work of these and the years immediately succeeding. For the problem he set for most of his early fictional rebels and victims was not so much one of politics or economics as of "art"—and not always in an especially broad sense of the word: the problem of preserving, against a brutal or sterile environment, a health in perceptivity, in feeling, in imagination. The reader is even inclined, and not without justice, to accuse the author of youthful preciosity and his characters of a fastidious artistic retreat before the essential disciplines of their civilization, the stone and steel upon which must be founded a life of the spirit.

Here the political commitments of Dos Passos provide something of the solid earthy context not always clearly established by the writings themselves. The wounds inflicted upon the protagonists can be recognized as the effect, within the most introspective reaches of the soul, of a specific social condition; the aestheticism of the author becomes a means of examining that condition at a particular spiritual level—the level at which consciousness is most keenly summed and concentrated—and a statement, in artistic terms, of the need for revolution. Nor can the audience of Dos Passos overlook the suggestion of irony with which he may have viewed the hero of *Three Soldiers*, and the possible hint that in the over-refined and undereducated sensibility of John Andrews lies one cause of Andrews's dilemma, his inability to grasp his situation or to take some positive stand toward the military machine until the very last.

Nevertheless, during this period the vantage point from which Dos Passos chose to study his society was that of aestheticism, and his judgments were so framed and expressed as to be those of an aesthete. He had not yet presented freedom as a concrete social force, possessed of a tradition and a method; his protagonists are obliged to preserve freedom within the secret recesses of their personalities and unite it to the most exquisite of their perceptions.

The tyranny of twentieth-century civilization appeared first in the major works of Dos Passos not in industrial but in military guise—though even prior to his army experience, as a student at Harvard, he had begun to establish a critical position toward his industrial surroundings.[2] The earliest of his novels of protest against the war spirit was

2. See Wrenn, pp. 99, 115, 146.

*One Man's Initiation—1917* (1920). More thorough in its argument is *Three Soldiers*, with its vivid analysis of the smothering of impulse and thought under the weight of military discipline. And the thing killed by army routine is the sensuous yet delicate experience of life that preoccupied so much of the thinking of Dos Passos at this time.

The section headings of the novel themselves suggest the process whereby living flesh and blood are treated as raw material to be transformed into serviceable, but wholly inexpressive and standardized, instruments of military use: "Making the Mould"; "The Metal Cools"; "Machines"; "Rust"—the wounded soldier as no more than a piece of corroded machinery, set aside by its users. In the section "The World Outside," the story relates the adventures of John Andrews during a period of temporary release from military duty, when he can again taste of life; "Under the Wheels" has him fleeing the army, and seized as a deserter.

The story of Andrews is told within a repeated imagery that conveys the machine-like method of the army. Andrews's early experience of the military suggests to him a rhythm "that expressed the dusty boredom, the harsh constriction of warm bodies full of gestures and attitudes and aspirations into moulds, like the moulds toy soldiers are cast in." Again, Andrews is gripped with despair at the probability that his life will go on indefinitely as a "slavery of unclean bodies packed together in places where the air had been breathed over and over, cogs in the great slow-moving Juggernaut of armies." Even though the fighting had stopped, the "armies would go on grinding out lives with lives, crushing flesh with flesh." The army is a thing of "tingling bodies constrained into the rigid attitudes of automatons in uniforms," a "hideous farce of making men into machines."[3]

3. *Three Soldiers* (New York: Random House, The Modern Library, 1932), pp. 17–18, 245, 360. Originally published in 1921.

The slavery against which Andrews protests is military, but there is in the novel an occasional implication that the war on freedom and the senses is conducted on a wider front, with differing modes of warfare, throughout modern civilization. Comparing the age of the Renaissance with his own, Andrews finds that the breadth and scope of individuality have lessened and society grown "arid." "Men seemed to have shrunk in stature before the vastness of the mechanical contrivances they had invented. . . . Today everything was congestion, the scurrying of crowds; men had become ant-like."[4]

And the accusation is directed more specifically at America. John Andrews dreams of the life that might be lived near to " 'the great rosy grey expanse' " of Paris, a " 'quiet mellow existence' " occupied with work and concerts; and contrasts this to his own life: " 'Slaving in that iron, metallic, brazen New York to write ineptitudes about music in the Sunday paper.' " " 'France is stifling,' said Andrews, all of a sudden. 'It stifles you very slowly, with beautiful silk bands. . . . America beats your brains out with a policeman's billy.' "[5] But such references to the machine, to modernity, and to America were as yet only secondary. It was the military that was for Dos Passos the embodiment of spiritual and sensual death.

Already the words of Dos Passos have given an indication of that quality of human experience he wished to have released from bondage to routine. The "warm bodies full of gestures and attitudes and aspirations," "tingling bodies," the serene existence a man could mold for himself in France, close to the beauty of Paris—all of this is on the plane of the sensuous and the aesthetic.

And the feeling is intensified. It is present when Andrews is pictured sitting "in a noisy café, full of yellow light flash-

4. *Ibid.*, p. 373.
5. *Ibid.*, pp. 254, 366.

ing in eyes and on glasses and bottles, of red lips crushed against the thin hard rims of glasses." Later, the reader finds Andrews, freed for the moment from army discipline, walking the streets of Paris, intoxicated by the luxuriant variety of impressions.

> He was walking very fast, stopping suddenly now and then to look at the greens and oranges and crimsons of vegetables in a push cart, to catch a vista down intricate streets, to look into the rich brown obscurity of a small wine shop where workmen stood at the counter sipping white wine. . . . [T]he faces of the people he passed moved him like rhythms of an orchestra.

Still under the spell of his release, Andrews realizes that he can now fill himself "with a reverberation of all the rhythms of men and women moving in the frieze of life before his eyes; no more like wooden automatons knowing only the motions of the drill manual, but supple and varied, full of force and tragedy."[6] It is in essence an artist's perceptions and an artist's desires that are extinguished in the world of military, and machine, repression.

*Three Soldiers* represents the tone of the author's first period. In American civilization as a whole he found a discipline at least analogous to that of the army, working destruction upon the same urges and sensitivities that are crushed in military routine. His protest forms the theme of "The Garbage Man."

The play tells of a lovers' quest; and the quest differs from that of John Andrews only in being more fanciful, less related to an aesthete's love of things that are richly and sensuously material. The lovers, Tom and Jane, are set against a series of backgrounds: an American town, a train stranded behind a wreck, and New York. In each situation,

6. *Ibid.*, pp. 254, 299, 313.

the vitality for which the girl and boy stand is opposed by
some element in their surroundings. The "Garbage Man"
himself reappears in differing forms throughout the play,
essentially as a symbol of death—toward which American
civilization tends.

At the outset of the drama, the antagonists are presented:
the lovers, and a work-driven society that aims to break
their waywardness and harness them to itself. Tom and
Jane are returning from a party. Tom exclaims:

> It's morning and we're both of us alive and not dead. It's
> morning and we've both of us got eyes and ears and noses to
> smell with and tongues to taste with
>     and lips to kiss. And we're full of ragtime and champagne
> punch and love and dancesteps and kisses. We're chockfull
> of dancing the way honey's full of sweet.

But the sound of engines in a powerplant interrupts their
joy.

JANE. Listen, they're angry at us.
TOM. They don't want us to be happy. They want us to be
shoveling coal, pounding typewriters, filling greasecups.

. . . . . . . . . . . . . . . . . . . .

JANE. They'd make us work till our hands couldn't feel
and our faces were gray and our eyes were blank. Tom, the
engine in the powerplant; that's all people. The engines are
made out of people pounded into steel. The power's stretched
on the muscles of people, the light's sucked out of people's
eyes.

As they go off the stage, "The rhythm of the powerplant
rises triumphant."

In the train-wreck scene, the machine appears as the
enemy to human flesh. And in the figure of a businessman,
impatient at the delay caused by the disaster, Dos Passos
emphasizes the relative cheapness in which a business

society holds life in comparison with the value it places upon money and upon the hoarding of time to gain it.

The battle between the human soul and an America dominated by business and the machine is quickened in the scenes set in New York. In an imagery of stock market tickers and 'clicking typewriters—pacing against the beat of Time, which will outlast its challengers—a "Telescope Man" in Union Square laments the undeviating concentration upon business, the relentless pace, that have taken from men the leisure and the interest to dream: to look at the moon through his telescope. Tom's words delineate an America of regimented activity among unresting minds, their attention disciplined, narrowed, fixed on a single set of abstractions.

> Concrete sprouting in sixteen dimensions, cogs and belts and gears multiplying sixteen by sixteen.
> Where's it all going?
> . . . . . . . . . . . . . . . . . .
> And the tides of people up and down through the worn grooves of the streets, over the polished asphalt.
> . . . . . . . . . . . . . . . .
> And always their eyes straight before them fastened on two times two.
> Their minds clicking like adding machines, their fingers itching for the round silver pieces, the crinkly green dollars.
> Walking lockstep.
> Shackled in Arrow Collar shackles.
> Crushing us.
> Making slaves of us.
> Making us walk lockstep.

The climax comes with a parade in which New York celebrates Prosperity. A "Voice of the Radio" expresses the spirit of the parade, praising the virtues of business and success-seeking, attacking dissenters. Breaking into full rebellion, Tom shouts, "Voice of the machine, voice of the machine, I defy you."

> It's not for you that the desires of men and women beat against the silver moon and temper it hard as a roaring gong by the beating of their wants.

He is pursued by the police.[7] But at the end Dos Passos grants the lovers a respite.

So the discipline of money and the machine had now replaced the discipline of armies as the adversary; but life, fresh and hungering, remained the sacrifice. The discipline itself had maintained its rigor and its clarity of structure, and could be exactly located at every point at which it touched upon explicitly depicted states of sensing and of artistic vision.

*Second Period: Manhattan Transfer, U. S. A.*

But notice that while the foreground of the play is sharp, the setting possesses its own drama. John Andrews's antagonist, the army, scarcely has a character or shape—except where it directly impinges on the liberty of the young soldier; the machine city of "The Garbage Man," to the contrary, constantly obtrudes itself as sound and gesticulation: the beat of the powerplant, the voice of the radio, the leap of tickers and cogs and gears.

In *Manhattan Transfer*, the setting is again forcefully present. The city dominates the novel: it is stage, protagonist, and villain. The human figures, even Jimmy Herf, seem significant not so much in themselves as in their relationship to Manhattan; each is introduced from time to time more to develop a situation than to fulfill his own person and story. Singly, each is a point of reference, making

7. *Three Plays* (New York: Harcourt, Brace and Company, 1934), pp. 4–5, 28–29, 46–47, 65–66, 68–73.

observation upon the city and at the same time personi-
fying the nerve and soul upon which Manhattan bears its
weight; together, they are the city, a cluster and tangle of
lives compacted into a single object. The technique, carried much further and relatively untouched by the almost
mystic character of the backgrounds to *Manhattan Transfer*, produced the solidity and mass of *U. S. A.*

In that work, the central evil has become more clearly
identifiable with capitalism. Yet "capitalism" is a term almost too narrow. Dos Passos was dealing with a total distortion in American life: a distortion of social powers that
was stifling American liberty; and a distortion of goals that
was stifling the personality, subordinating ideal and creative instinct to the pursuit of success.[8] As in *Manhattan
Transfer*, the nucleus remains the individual—J. Ward
Moorehouse and Richard Savage, who succumb to their
environment, or Ben Compton and Mary French, who com-
bat it, or Joe Williams and Anne Elizabeth Trent, who are
its victims; and the treatment can be in its own way as
introspective as in the early work of Dos Passos. But again,
as in *Manhattan Transfer*, the sense of mass and volume
is pronounced—more so. It is carried in the great multi-
tude of characters; in the interweaving of plot with historical context, and the continental stage upon which the
story is played; at the end of the trilogy, in the perception
of a libertarian impulse; in the very bulk of *U. S. A.* itself.

Occasionally *U. S. A.* appears to revert to the problem of
technological discipline. Allusions are made in "The American Plan" and "Tin Lizzie"—sketches of Frederick Wins-
low Taylor and Henry Ford. While crediting Taylor with
an honest willingness, unshared by the owners, to see men

8. T. K. Whipple has identified the moral condition of the times as the
central concern of the story, with the class struggle as secondary. *Study
Out the Land* (Berkeley and Los Angeles: University of California Press,
1943), pp. 86–87.

paid for good labor, Dos Passos represented Taylorism as a system for the attainment of wealth through the sacrifice of thought and expression to an increased intensity of work. And here is the speedup at the Ford enterprise: "... reach under, adjust washer, screw down bolt, shove in cotterpin, reachunder adjustwasher, screwdown bolt, reachunderadjustscrewdownreachunderadjust until every ounce of life was sucked off into production and at night the workmen went home grey shaking husks. . . ."[9]

The placing of these passages, however, provides an illustration of the new emphasis. Both appear in *The Big Money*, the final of the three novels, which carries the tale through the flush times of the nineteen twenties, and both are set in a portion of the novel that follows the story of Charley Anderson, a promising aviator and technician whose pursuit of the big money brings personal disintegration. The indictment, therefore, is not of the machine itself: to the contrary, for in a purer service to technology Anderson might have found salvation. The evils of the speedup express chiefly the false ends and methods of business.

It is an enemy more broadly defined than that which had confronted John Andrews in *Three Soldiers* or the youthful lovers of "The Garbage Man," and the setting and cast of characters have been widened also. It remained for Dos Passos to reframe his conception of freedom to fit the new perspective of *U. S. A.*, and this he did. Freedom as it appears in the trilogy is no longer simply the possession, by a private soul, of its own sensations and intuitions. It is a concrete, forceful thrust against the physical as well as the mental instruments of oppression; and it expresses itself in a distinct American people and tradition.

In Bartolomeo Vanzetti, Dos Passos saw reflected the story of America's founding by other immigrant foes of

9. *The Big Money*, pp. 19–25, 55; in *U. S. A.* (New York: Random House, The Modern Library, 1939).

tyranny. Writing of Vanzetti, Dos Passos scanned the power of the American tradition of liberty and the mighty extent of the continent on which it spread itself from its landing at Plymouth:

> this is where the immigrants landed the roundheads the sackers of castles the kingkillers haters of oppression this is where they stood in a cluster after landing from the crowded ship that stank of bilge      on the beach that belonged to no one      between the ocean that belonged to no one and the enormous forest that belonged to no one that stretched over the hills where the deertracks were up the green river-valleys where the redskins grew their tall corn in patches forever into the incredible west
>
> for threehundred years the immigrants toiled into the west. . . .

America needs a reawakening of the words of liberty once spoken by the Plymouth immigrants and now corrupted by the agents of oppression; for without the words,

> how can you know who are your betrayers America
> or that this fishpeddler you have in Charlestown Jail is one of your founders Massachusetts?[10]

The I.W.W. in particular revealed the untamed spirit to which Dos Passos looked for the rejuvenation of the country:

> Along the coast in cookshacks flophouses jungles wobblies hoboes bindlestiffs began singing Joe Hill's songs. They sang 'em in the county jails of the State of Washington, Oregon, California, Nevada, Idaho, in the bullpens in Montana and Arizona, sang 'em in Walla Walla, San Quentin and Leavenworth,
>
> forming the structure of the new society within the jails of the old.[11]

10. *Ibid.*, pp. 435–437.
11. *Nineteen Nineteen*, p. 422; in *U. S. A.*

*Third Period: Adventures of a Young Man,*
*The Ground We Stand On, Later Works*

Dos Passos still had elaborations to make upon his representation of American liberty. Even in the year of publication of *The Big Money*, he was sufficiently reconciled to
the course of things that he could vote for Roosevelt, then
seeking his second presidential term. As the decade of the
thirties drew to a close, Dos Passos became completely
estranged from the Communist movement—the estrange-
ment found its literary expression in *Adventures of a Young
Man*; and he was basically at peace with America's dominant institutions—or at any rate, as reformed by the New
Deal administrations. But if the existing order was no
longer one of enslavement, he could no longer cast the de-
fenders of freedom so clearly in the role of rebels against
their environment. Freedom was, in truth, the environment,
and must therefore be defined in its more peaceful character.[12]

The new definition can be found in *Adventures of a
Young Man*. Here, in an American "primer of liberties,"
Dos Passos set down the hard-headed principles that for
him were the American answer to communism, among
them, that freedom must be bought by vigilance, self-de-
nial, and "the canny weighing of political prospects," and
that "means are more important than ends, because means
mould institutions which frame ways of behaving, while
ends are never in any man's lifetime attained. . . ."[13] In

12. While his affirmation of the unique American experience became
increasingly pronounced in his later works, even in the late nineteen
twenties Dos Passos was adhering to a brand of leftwing deviationism
that he termed "American exceptionalism." See "Reminiscences of a Middle-Class Radical, II," *National Review*, I (February 15, 1956), 10.

13. *Adventures of a Young Man*, p. 342; in *District of Columbia* (Boston: Houghton Mifflin Company, 1952).

*The Ground We Stand On,* Dos Passos placed the habit of political sobriety at the very center of the great self-governing tradition of the English-speaking nations. "Politics is our whole history. . . . By politics I mean simply the art of inducing people to behave in groups with a minimum of force and bloodshed." The tribal traditions within which the common law is rooted had just that purpose: "the patching up of private and public rows without violence by the opinion of a jury or the counting of heads at a meeting." Our answer to "deathdealing illusions" should be an increased application of self-government to factories, unions, and the other institutions of modern life.[14]

Even in this more recent phase of his thinking, Dos Passos does not portray an American libertarian tradition characterized by qualities of restraint and practicality alone —energetic, expansive traits suggest themselves still. Americans, he has written, are still frontiersmen, and compared with communities across the seas, "even our oldest cities are the provisional bivouacs of a raw and fluid civilization that has not yet stiffened into a frame." And America has offered

> exultation
> in the windy freedom of a continent

Gusty and yet politically wise, American liberty struggles in the pages of the later works of Dos Passos to assert itself against specific totalitarian opponents, but more basically against the tendency to totalitarian concentration of power that the author takes to be inherent in any advanced industrial society.[15]

14. *The Ground We Stand On: Some Examples from the History of a Political Creed* (New York: Harcourt, Brace and Company, 1941), pp. 8, 12.

15. *State of the Nation* (Boston: Houghton Mifflin Company, 1944), p. 5; *The Grand Design* (1949), p. 443; in *District of Columbia; The Prospect Before Us* (Boston: Houghton Mifflin Company, 1950), pp. 7–8.

# Chapter 5

# Thorstein Veblen
# and Carl Sandburg

## IN AFFIRMATION OF THE MACHINE

THE work of Sherwood Anderson and Waldo Frank, along with the earlier writings of Dos Passos, was disposed toward condemnation of the disciplines of the machine. Yet within a world ordered by machines and their technology there is an austerity that possesses its own appeal, aesthetic as well as moral. Especially in Anderson's novels and studies we have seen the evidence of that appeal—and upon an artist peculiarly representative of the literary protest against the "Puritan" temper of American life. Obliquely and often hesitatingly acknowledged in Anderson's work, the ascetic virtues of the intellect disciplined by the machine receive vigorously sympathetic treatment at the hands of Thorstein Veblen.

Veblen was preoccupied with the most rationalistic values of machine society. His work may be compared with the poetry of Carl Sandburg, whose lyric temper has responded to those things in democratic industrial America that are forceful, impetuous, in ferment. Through the extremity of their contrast, the interpretations of machine culture provided by Sandburg and Veblen present a vision of the age that is an intensification of that with which we have been dealing: energy and discipline are fixed at the poles of the modern technological spirit.

### THORSTEIN VEBLEN

At a time that such rebels as Lester Ward were breaking the established patterns of economic thought, Thorstein Veblen hastened the pace of revolt. And he offered a clearly original economics, a distinct alternative to the older, Marxist critique of laissez-faire economy.

As an economist in rebellion, Veblen was even more effective because of the flexibility and suggestiveness that are among the most noticeable characteristics of his thinking. Had he attempted to present a complete system, rigid and internally consistent as the economics of Marx or Adam Smith, it might have been a second-rate system, soon forgotten—or a new orthodoxy, to be followed in time by a new revolt. Instead he offered hints, a stimulus to further investigation, and a scepticism highly acid in its effect upon received economic doctrine.

Most important, Veblen worked toward a greater subtlety in the psychology of economics. Setting aside the assumption of classical liberalism that in economic affairs every man behaves about the same, acting upon calculation of cost and profit, Veblen believed that every economic order (and every differing part of a single order) might have as its origin and its effect some distinctive "discipline" of personality, enforcing upon the individual particular standards of workmanship and desire and even metaphysical thought. Indeed, his detection of an "instinct of workmanship" was itself a considerable modification of the pleasure-pain psychology maintained by the classical economists.

It follows that an economy cannot be studied as a total mechanism, harmonious or strained within by the workings of self-interested desire, but must be examined more closely to see the concrete way in which its members think and labor, the concrete and unique goals even of their self-interest, and the conflicting "disciplines" that may exist within the system. *The Theory of the Leisure Class* (1899), for example, is a study in economic psychology, an investigation into the irrationalities that determine the criteria of leisure and consumption; and the main burden of Veblen's work is a demonstration that the mental training given by business is starkly different from that given by the machine.

Throughout, Veblen's method was analytical, nominalist, and corrosive to the belief in total economic schemes; yet, while his thought remained pliable and free of an overly confining systematization, it took a number of partial stands. Among the most familiar is, again, the distinction between the business and the technological components of the modern economy: a distinction that Veblen sharpened by his own preference for the workwise abilities and attitudes of the technician. But Veblen's argument cannot be understood without reference to the "instinct of workmanship," a category of consciousness from which he could derive standards for the evaluation of different kinds of human activity.

## The Instinct of Workmanship

Veblen did not establish in any comprehensive way the psychological origins of the instinct of workmanship—whether as a pre-existent mental form, or a synthesis of instincts, or a product of social environment. His definition of the instinct itself, moreover, was of considerable breadth. Veblen apparently had in mind the complex of human tastes and commitments that attend, not the ulterior objectives of life—for these are laid down by the other instincts and desires—but all the widely varied deeds by which those objectives are attained. As Veblen wrote in *The Theory of the Leisure Class*, man sees himself as "a centre of unfolding impulsive activity—'teleological' activity," an agent incessantly seeking the achievement of ends.

> By force of his being such an agent he is possessed of a taste for effective work, and a distaste for futile effort. He has a sense of the merit of serviceability or efficiency and of the demerit of futility, waste, or incapacity. This aptitude or prospensity may be called the instinct of workmanship.[1]

In his study *The Instinct of Workmanship*, Veblen made it clear that he was speaking of a human appetite for ways and means that is quite separate from the concern for ends.

> Yet workmanship is none the less an object of attention and sentiment in its own right. Efficient use of the means at hand and adequate management of the resources available for the purposes of life is itself an end of endeavour, and accomplishment of this kind is a source of gratification.[2]

So identified, the instinct of workmanship takes on several important characteristics. First, its expression is an "object of attention and sentiment," a "source of gratifica-

1. *The Theory of the Leisure Class: An Economic Study in the Evolution of Institutions* (New York: The Macmillan Company; London: Macmillan and Company, 1899), p. 15.
2. *The Instinct of Workmanship and the State of the Industrial Arts* (Copyright 1914 by Macmillan Company, 1942 by Ann B. Sims. All rights reserved. Reprinted by permission of The Viking Press, Inc.), pp. 31–32.

tion"; the instinct has a value all its own, and the society that can most fully nourish it—whatever ultimate goals that society may set for itself—possesses a large measure of health. Man's approval of useful activity and his scorn of waste and futility, Veblen said elsewhere, are closely related both to the ethical and to the aesthetic norms of conduct, and he spoke of the technician's "responsibility to his own sense of workmanlike performance, which might well be called the engineer's conscience."[3]

Also, the instinct is quite plainly of a scope beyond that included under the artistic instinct of craft—or at any rate, of craft as some of its romantic advocates would seem to conceive it. It will be recalled that Sherwood Anderson thought of craftsmanship as a sensuous experience of life through the fingers (though he made a place for the machine technician—as well as for the literary artist); and it is in manual dexterity, combined with a certain mental playfulness and turned to the making of beautiful things, that romantics would locate their ideal of craft. But whenever a challenging objective is established and materials are competently manipulated to reach it, Veblen's instinct of workmanship has been called to life. The point is significant: it means that Veblen was prepared to discover in acts far removed from those of craftsmanship, narrowly defined, a moral and aesthetic dimension highly similar to that often assigned to craft alone. A way is opened to an appreciation of machine technology on its own terms, if it can be seen to quicken in its attendants the workman's instinct, and to discipline them to clear-headed and effective methods of labor.

3. *Essays in Our Changing Order*, edited by Leon Ardzrooni (New York: The Viking Press, 1934), pp. 81–82; *Absentee Ownership and Business Enterprise in Recent Times: The Case of America* (Copyright 1923 by B. W. Huebsch, Inc., 1951 by Ann B. Sims. Reprinted by permission of The Viking Press, Inc.), p. 107.

Here another of the fundamentals of Veblen's thought needs clarification—his employment of the term "discipline." By the expression, which recurs frequently and in a variety of contexts, he meant the workings of any environment in shaping the mind and the habits of the men who must live under its sway and, more especially, in determining their character as workmen. There can scarcely be any human community within these terms that is not subjected to some discipline, perhaps quite demanding in its own right.

When Veblen dealt with the discipline imposed upon humankind by the technology of the machine he was therefore employing a concept of discipline applicable in some fashion to every social ordering, and the discipline of machine industry cannot by its mere existence lay claim to an ascetic rigor peculiarly its own. But however Veblen might compare it in point of intensity to the conditionings of human life brought about by other environments, the discipline of the machine does in his description assume a striking severity and demonstrates an unusual capacity to toughen the rational faculties: to train those faculties in the accurate understanding of the materials that are to be molded by the workman into new forms or skillfully guided along their own course, and to teach the laborer exactness in work. The nature and the extent of that discipline, as it appears in Veblen's interpretation, become apparent when it is contrasted to what Veblen depicted as the regime of the handicraft period in early modern times.

## The Discipline of Handicraft

Veblen's handicraftsman was not the simple poet and joyful free spirit whose demise some modern artists and intellectuals have lamented. He was essentially a good burgher, half artisan, half businessman. He seems more closely linked to the present world than to the medieval; the craft era merged by degrees into the era of the machine.

The distinctive feature of the craftsman's work, Veblen demonstrated, was the dominant position it assigned to the worker in relation to his task. If at this point we carry Veblen's argument a step or two beyond the limits at which his own words left it, what may we conclude of the craftsman and his labors? Certainly not that he was free of constraint. He had to submit to the manifold and unbending properties of matter; he encountered the rigid specifications demanded of the final product. Since the work of the handicraft era was of the highest quality, it is to be presumed that properties and specifications were fully respected. But beyond these, the work had no power over the worker. The labor was not paced, nor was the job finely connected, in a sequence of time or event, with a larger process; the materials lay inert, at the craftsman's mercy. There existed a wide latitude within which, if he could not perpetrate error, he was nonetheless at liberty to muddle through from provisional error to perfected accomplishment. While Veblen never marked out in this manner the craftsman's powers and his freedoms, the freedoms are the logical converse of the unique bounds within which Veblen's machine technician is held, and their positing should give a greater clarity to his total argument.

The craft worker, moreover, was trained to a particular understanding of the phenomena he observed and employed; he saw in operation there the same relationship of cause to result as was his relationship to his own creations. The cause was viewed as controlling and imparting its own character to the effect.

The cause is the producer, the effect the product. Relatively little emphasis or interest falls upon the process out of which the product emerges; the interest being centred upon the latter and its relation to the efficient cause out of which it has come. . . . The cause "makes" the effect,

much as the craftsman is perceived to make an article.[4]

A further result is that existence was seen to work itself out in episodic fashion, as a craftsman enacts episodes of creation. For every event, the scientific investigator searched for one efficient cause, which was presumed to dominate and beside which the remaining conditioning circumstances could be no more than accessory. "The inquiry looked to the beginning and end of an episode of activity," resulting in a finished product.

> The craftsman is the agency productively engaged in the case, while his tools and materials are accessories to his force and skill, and the finished goods leave his hands as an end achieved; and so an episode of creative efficiency is rounded off.[5]

This idea of the natural order has prevailed until recently in the investigations of modern science.

## The Discipline of the Machine

In the technology of the machine, the relation between the worker and the process of work is reversed. The techniques and the motions are established by the machine, to which the industrial laborer must adapt himself; in effect, he is to the machine as the tool was to the craftsman. And the machine process is itself of a nature peculiarly to condition the thinking and the reflexes of those who tend it. Within the factory and throughout the closely integrated economy of an industrial society the process consists of an

4. *The Theory of Business Enterprise* (New York: Charles Scribner's Sons, 1904), pp. 365–366.
5. *The Instinct of Workmanship*, pp. 324–325.

unbroken and unending series of events, tightly conjoined and exactly timed, so that any maladjustment of part to part, any minute failure at adaptation by the worker, the technician, or the administrator will disrupt the whole; the system thus makes a constant and pressing demand upon the thought of all responsible for its maintenance.

> The whole concert of industrial operations is to be taken as a machine process, made up of interlocking detail processes, rather than as a multiplicity of mechanical appliances each doing its particular work in severalty. This comprehensive industrial process draws into its scope and turns to account all branches of knowledge that have to do with the material sciences. . . .[6]

Veblen insisted that the discipline of the machine falls, not only upon its technicians and workmen, but in lesser degree upon every citizen of an industrial state. Here, as within the factory, is a delicately adjusted and closely timed sequence of events, to which the consumer must accommodate himself as the worker is paced to the machine process:

> To take effectual advantage of what is offered as the wheels of routine go round, in the way of work and play, livelihood and recreation, he must know by facile habituation what is going on and how and in what quantities and at what price and where and when, and for the best effect he must adapt his movements with skilled exactitude and a cool mechanical insight to the nicely balanced moving equilibrium of the mechanical processes engaged. To live—not to say at ease— under the exigencies of this machine-made routine requires a measure of consistent training in the mechanical apprehension of things. The mere mechanics of conformity to the schedule of living implies a degree of trained insight and a facile strategy in all manner of quantitative adjustments and

6. *The Theory of Business Enterprise*, pp. 7–8.

adaptations, particularly at the larger centres of population, where the routine is more comprehensive and elaborate.[7]

Modern technology is also present in any industry, including that of agriculture, that has turned from manual dexterity and rule of thumb to precise and reasoned procedure.[8]

The conduct of work and life has been reordered, and with it the judgment of phenomena. Since the worker is no longer a craftsman, he will not impute to events a law of causation analogous to the method of craft, with its observable progression from maker to product. Furthermore, by its own power of analogy mechanical technology suggests a new conception of nature. "The machine technology"—by which Veblen could have meant with equal reason the theoretical science and technique of the modern age, the scheme of the machine and the factory, or the greater but comparable scheme that subsists within the total economic and social mechanism—"is a mechanical or material process, and requires the attention to be centred upon this process and the exigencies of the process." Because the process operates as a continuous flow, the distinction between prime efficient cause and its effect becomes obliterated: the technologist "learns to think in terms of the process, rather than in terms of a productive cause and a product between which the process intervenes in such a manner as to afford a transition from one to the other."[9] The sense of causation is not exactly discarded: it is reinterpreted, so that the episodic universe of the earlier modern scientists, the universe that progresses through discrete causal impulses, is transformed into a total unfold-

7. *The Instinct of Workmanship*, pp. 311–314.
8. *The Theory of Business Enterprise*, p. 6, and footnote 1, pp. 6–7.
9. *Ibid.*, pp. 367–368.

ing act.[10] Continuous sequence and quantitative measurement become the new terms and devices of technological and scientific inquiry.

Veblen would have to agree, then, with those nostalgic traditionalists who find the essential characteristic of mechanical technology to be its subordination of the worker to the machine. But paradoxically, this subordination appears in Veblen's analysis as the basis not of mental atrophy but of seasoned intelligence.

As has been noted, the special responsibilities of skill and initiative assumed by the craftsman undoubtedly carried with them, in compensation, a large measure of freedom and safety. Neither in the job, nor in the materials upon which the worker labored, nor in the larger economic situation in which he was placed, did there exist any power of motion independent of his own, or any pressing demand beyond the specifications of the particular work at hand. Under the regime of machine technology, the materials and the total environment move from the passive to the active role; they therefore call forth a new kind of response from men. In its intricacy and in the exactness of its synchronization, the machine process will admit of no lack in knowledge, no failure in logic, not the slightest slackening of concentration on the part of those who subserve it. The fine old skills of the craftsman will no longer do, and a different set of skills and abilities must take their place: analytical logic, a regard for precision, the mastery of a large body of technical information, a trained and self-possessed alertness that can cope with events in swift and intricate series.

These new aptitudes, Veblen believed, would form the essential character of man in a machine society. In *The*

10. *The Instinct of Workmanship*, pp. 325–326.

*Instinct of Workmanship,* he told of "the increasingly exacting requirements of the machine industry, particularly
in the way of accurate, alert and facile conformity to the
requirements of the machine process," and of the expanding need in a machine society for lengthy education of the
young;[11] and in *The Nature of Peace,* he wrote that "every
appreciable technological advance presumes, as a requisite
to its working-out in industry, an augmented state of information and of logical facility in the workmen under whose
hands it is to take effect."[12] And we have seen that Veblen
would consider the modern talents of intellect a necessity
for every detail of life; like the factory hand and the technician, the consumer must call upon a "skilled exactitude
and a cool mechanical insight," a "facile strategy."

In still another fashion, it would seem, the machine provides a schooling in good workmanship: it refines the worker's comprehension of phenomena. The instincts, Veblen
argued, do not exist in isolation. Each is subject to "con-
tamination" from the rest, and the instinct of workmanship
is no less vulnerable than the other elements in the human
personality; any number of predispositions might stand
between the workman and a perfect knowledge of his materials or his techniques. Remarkable among these distor-
tions is the "self-contamination" of the instinct, when the
worker, precisely because he is so conscious of his own experience in labor, reads a corresponding experience into
the minute workings of matter. In so doing, he becomes
incapable of coming wholly to grips with the sequences
of natural events on their own terms; yet it is with these
sequences that he must deal if he is to construct a highly

11. *Ibid.,* pp. 306–310, and footnote 1, pp. 309–310.
12. *An Inquiry into the Nature of Peace and the Terms of Its Perpetuation* (Copyright 1917 by Macmillan Company, 1945 by Ann B. Sims.
Reprinted by permission of The Viking Press, Inc.), p. 335.

advanced technology, although Veblen did recognize that in most societies, with their relatively simple technical equipments, the preconception would not constitute a serious hindrance to the work immediately at hand. A particular instance of this "self-contamination" would be, of course, the thought of the handicraft period,[13] with its law of episodic cause and effect. And while Veblen was not very definite on the point, he appeared to credit highly the technology of the machine for its success in hardening man's perception of the material world and teaching him a subtler understanding of causal sequence.

The argument is curious, and perhaps must be counted among the less trustworthy of Veblen's constructions. It is a layman's perilous attempt at explication—and more dangerously, at evaluation—of conflicting and rapidly evolving scientific hypotheses upon the nature of causality. Its formulation, moreover, lacks something in the way of lucidity. The reader is never quite made aware whether the machine process that teaches the new lesson of sequence embraces, as elsewhere in Veblen's writing, the interlocked mechanism of the factory, and beyond, the mechanism of the modern economy, or whether it includes only the process as it is more narrowly examined by the theoretical technician and the scientist. Veblen would doubtless insist that the distinction is unnecessary and that each element in the machine process is involved; but a closer definition of his subject might have strengthened the presentation. Finally, by its very scope and character Veblen's thesis cannot look to extensive psychological documentation and can only be considered a bold guess. But as a restatement of his more general thesis—that the intricate sequence of events within a machine economy drills the intellect in

13. *The Instinct of Workmanship*, pp. 242–243.

objectivity and unlimbers certain analytical powers—it possesses at the very least a value as drama and as illustration.

## The Discipline of Business

Set against his examination of the handicraft era, Veblen's analysis of machine civilization makes an emphatic case for the disciplines of machine technology and the workmanlike virtues of its attendants. Another contrast of greater polemical interest to Veblen was that of the disciplines of business to those of the machine. It was in the working out of this distinction that he committed himself most positively to the cause of the technician, as a workman and as the fitting commander of a machine economy. Veblen's discussion of the businessman may be broken down into two parts: his identification of the place held by the entrepreneur within the modern economy and his investigation into the business mentality.

The station of the businessman, Veblen found, is at those points in the machine process where there is a potential gap between the elements that make it up. His role is one of "interstitial adjustment" among highly interdependent technical and economic components—more specifically, adjustment between a concern and its employees, and between different concerns. Because the industrial process must be of a perfect continuity if it is to function properly, its fate is delicately balanced at its points of juncture, and the slightest disruption could extend its ill effects far within the system. As it happens, the businessman who can effect such a disruption may in many instances stand to gain from it a "differential advantage."[14] But it is not only the self-interest of the businessman, as he was conceived

14. *The Theory of Business Enterprise*, pp. 18–19, 25–28.

by Veblen, that sets him at odds with the modern technological system. The discipline under which he is trained forms within him a mentality ill-fitted to the demands of the machine.

In Veblen's description, the discipline of business is a complex of values and methods of conduct founded in part in the conditions of the handicraft period. From the nature of craft, for example, came the Lockean theory of property ownership.[15] Yet business has passed beyond the tutelage of craft, and its own exigencies discipline human character in a number of attitudes that stand in direct opposition to those of the technician. The skills of the businessman are the skills, not of mechanical logic and precise quantitative observation, but of salesmanship, of canniness and worldly shrewdness. "The captain of industry is an astute man rather than an ingenious one, and his captaincy is a pecuniary rather than an industrial captaincy"— if some exception be made for the early captains, among whom were technicians of real merit.[16] Or to state the case differently, the standards of business act as one of the "contaminations" of the instinct of workmanship, "so that even the serviceability of any given action or policy for the common good comes to be rated in terms of the pecuniary gain which such conduct will bring to its author."[17]

Inexpert in the industrial arts and hostile to their free working, the businessman could be scarcely more than an incubus upon a mature machine economy. In his later writing, Veblen became increasingly cutting in his attack upon the business community and began to make extensive use of the term "sabotage" with reference to the deliberate

15. *Ibid.*, pp. 77–79.
16. *The Theory of the Leisure Class*, p. 230; *The Engineers and the Price System* (New York: B. W. Huebsch, 1921), pp. 32–33.
17. *The Instinct of Workmanship*, pp. 217–218.

efforts of business, and labor, to disrupt the economy; he used the word in its classic connotation, in which it means any attempt at hindrance or willful inefficiency. He also drew more distinctly the battle lines between the businessman and the conscientious technologist, so that *The Engineers and the Price System* (1921) reads almost like a call for the overthrow of capitalism by a soviet of technicians. The new society that Veblen at this time was hopefully envisioning would be one in which fact-minded engineers, impatient of waste and indirection, would be given a free hand to operate the economy in accordance with their workmanlike tastes; as an inevitable result, the public would enjoy a material abundance. For this dream the name of Veblen has become indissolubly associated with the idea of "technocracy."

The distinction between business and the machine sets the work of Veblen apart from some of the more literary interpretations that his younger contemporaries advanced as they explored their industrial America. To be sure, the ascetic scientists of Lewis's *Arrowsmith* brood in lonely laboratories, insulated as far as possible from the commercial world, but they are pure theoreticians, as estranged from technological as from pecuniary concerns; and in *Dodsworth*, with its entrepreneurial hero who has presided with earnest competence over the manufacture of automobiles, technology and business are fused. In the works of other authors, the two ranks of industrial society seem to merge as a single entity, against which the sensitive spirit must wage its war for a freer self-expression. And it remains a question whether, even within the basic terms of Veblen's own thought, the distinction need have been made so acute.

The place that Veblen assigned the businessman within the structure of the machine economy is itself, it might be supposed, squarely within the domain of the machine and

its discipline. The business representative mans the interstices in the machine process, where the many sub-proc-
esses must be gathered and meticulously combined. But
if so, his position should relate him to the larger process as
the technician is related to the factory, the worker to the
assembly line, or the commuter to the subway train; the
elements with which he must deal, the rhythmed schedule
to which they move, the precision demanded of their adjustment, are essentially in character with the process as it
exists at any of its points. Even if Veblen be granted his
debatable assumption that the businessman profits in considerable part from maladjustments rather than smooth
functionings of the system, and it be further acknowledged
that these require less workmanlike finesse than would a
synchronization exactly adapted to highest productivity,
surely the disruption must itself be planned by a calculation that analyzes in some general way the intricate composition of the economic system that is to be disrupted.
Only by such calculation could the disturbance be so con-
trolled as to benefit its architect.

As an example, a price war might involve the most sensitive reckonings upon the technological needs of the com-
peting firms, the prices that are required if these needs are
to be fulfilled, the extent of the technological damage to
each competitor from a temporary fall in revenue, and the
magnitude of the differential advantage to be gained by
the victor. If the business leader has his subordinates to
whom these questions are referred, the questions themselves are nevertheless inextricably involved in the situation, and the industrial captain must recognize their
relevance. He must respect and take into account the sub-
tleties of the machine process, for ultimately it encom-
passes his fate as it does that of the laborers and engineers
who tend it.

Veblen also neglected to explain the method by which

the "interstices" within the economy would be managed under a regime of engineers. Undoubtedly, many superfluous business positions—sinecures, perhaps, or jobs wholly concerned with salesmanship—would disappear; with the reordering of the economy, the location of the junction points might shift; and the new industrial managers, with their unconditional devotion to productivity, would fix their attention more closely upon the machine process, that it might be made to work precisely to its legitimate end. But Veblen did not demonstrate that in its fundamental nature—its basic techniques and the economic materials to which these techniques must be applied—the work of "interstitial adjustment" within a civilization of engineers would impose upon its servants a discipline radically different from that to which the business executives are subjected. To facilitate the allocation of supplies, one would suppose, the economic technicians might even adopt a scheme of price.

Veblen in fact acknowledged that business is to some degree subject to the discipline of the machine. In *The Theory of Business Enterprise*, he observed that even the bankers, lawyers, and brokers whose occupations are especially remote from tools and machines must give some consideration to

> the mechanical apparatus of everyday life; they are at least compelled to take some thought of what may be called the mechanics of consumption. Whereas those business men whose business is more immediately concerned with industry commonly have some knowledge and take some thought of the processes of industry; to some appreciable extent they habitually think in mechanical terms.[18]

Veblen was seldom even this generous; yet upon one score he conceded the existence, within business, of a discipline

18. *The Theory of Business Enterprise*, pp. 316–317.

that is of strongly mechanical or quasi-mechanical character. He referred to the system of accountancy.

A creation of the price system, accountancy requires
that phenomena be analyzed in their impersonal, quantitative dimensions, Veblen argued; its method and its point
of view are therefore analogous to the method and outlook
of technology. Accountancy "makes immediately for an
exact quantitative apprehension of all things and relations
that have a pecuniary bearing; and more remotely, by
force of the pervasive effect of habituation, it makes for a
greater readiness to apprehend all facts in a similarly objective and statistical fashion, in so far as the facts admit
of a quantitative rating." Accountancy is "of an extremely
dispassionate and impartially exacting nature"; and in the
training it gives in the coldly impersonal understanding of
fact, the price system has undoubtedly aided in the development of machine technology.[19] And from a marriage
of the disciplines that are given in accountancy and in the
machine has come the most refined expression of the modern spirit: the "higher learning" of the machine age.

The argument is set down in *The Higher Learning in
America*. The more controversial theme of the work concerns the conflict between the intellectual aims of university life and the business and commercial practices that
are imposed upon the university by the businessmen who
fill its administrative posts. The study reflects Veblen's
basic animosity toward the business mind; it is also in part
an expression of Veblen's personal war against university
bureaucracy. But beyond its immediate polemic, *The
Higher Learning* aims at a definition of the modern temper of scholarship and an explanation of its origins.

19. *The Instinct of Workmanship*, pp. 244–245; *The Higher Learning
in America: A Memorandum on the Conduct of Universities by Business
Men* (New York: B. W. Huebsch, 1918), p. 7.

Any system of knowledge, Veblen claimed, springs mainly from two human traits: the instinct of workmanship and the "idle curiosity"—a curiosity that seeks knowledge without regard for its uses. The instinct of workmanship is involved because it establishes the criteria by which fact is interpreted. Machine technology and accountancy further a method of inquiry that is severely impersonal and that does not place a personal value upon the information it discovers. Even though the technician may have as his practical object the fulfilling of some material human need, in his investigations he views phenomena exactly and dispassionately, submits to the dry truths he discovers and accepts them on their own terms. The impulse carries over into the realm of scholarship and speculation and there is brought to highest fruition, abandoning even the utilitarian objectives of the workman. Whereas in the Middle Ages knowledge was valued chiefly for its usefulness—even religion was considered mainly as a pragmatic means to salvation—learning is honored in our day as an end of human endeavor, and it is quested as chastely as the scientist scans the facts of his mechanical world. The "idle curiosity" has come into its own.[20]

The hard technological personality delineated by Veblen has fitted itself to the complexities of its mechanical world and moves within these with singleness of purpose and a cool brain. Here is a good workman, exact in analysis of his materials, sophisticated in his grasp of the causal sequence within which they are linked, facile in manipulating them to chosen ends. It may be assumed that in his labors, the universal aesthetic and moral components in the instinct of workmanship come to fulfilled expression; but in addition, his stripped logic and methods betoken the modern

20. *The Higher Learning*, pp. 5–7, 10, 34–35, 76.

functionalist aesthetic. Through the medium of economic thought, Veblen discovered the artist-technician whom Anderson discerned through the medium of poetic imagination.

## CARL SANDBURG

Veblen spoke for the strain of scientific rationalism in the machine personality; Carl Sandburg represents the Whitmanesque tradition in the temperament of industrial democracy. And therefore his poetry interprets an industrial world radically distinct from that of Veblen: immense and roughly formed where Veblen's was crisp and ordered, romantic where Veblen's was factual. Disciplined technological man obliquely makes his appearance in Sandburg's poems, but he is not isolated from the poetic background.

The poetry creates at least two distinguishable moods. In one, Sandburg presents a cosmos that is misty and elusive in its meanings—the workmanship of a giving but impenetrable Deity—and a people who take on the quality of their dark-shrouded surroundings. Great movements of men are perceived, but not as rank and fleshly masses— more nearly as spirits moved by dreams toward goals dimly intuited or unknown. Here the skyscraper becomes a technological sign of their searching. The other mood of the poems is more earthy. No longer a spirit-people carrying the burden of their hopes and their imaginings into the infinity of darkness that envelops them, the people are now forcefully, boisterously writing their hopes and imaginings into the customs, the governments, the steel and concrete of civilization. And here the machine becomes the sign of their force. But in both characters, the people are beyond proportioned form; they are in vast and shifting shapes.

Especially in some of his earlier work Sandburg connoted the lonely obscurity of the universe in which he was to cast his searching mankind. The title poem in *Slabs of the Sunburnt West* (1922) speaks of the faint message that reaches the senses, the " 'five sleepwalkers,' " from the cosmos they explore:

> "They go out, look, listen, wonder, and shoot a fire-white rocket across the night sky; the shot and the flare of the rocket dies to a whisper; and the night is the same as it always was."

The word they carry back is " '*Wait*.' " Through the night and the mist wander a people mysterious as the dark itself —and vast in outline even when man seems most vulnerable within the infinite setting. The shadowy bulk of the people looms largest in *The People, Yes* (1936): the endless movement of the sea and the wind suggest the unquenchable wanting of man; and the depth of the sea, in which mountains are buried, is the measure of "the toss and drip of the mystery of the people."[21]

Recurrent in the poems is an image concordant with Sandburg's spirit-world—an image of skyscrapers at night. Appearing as early as "Skyscraper," in the *Chicago Poems* (1916), the imagery is repeated in "Prayers of Steel," published in *Cornhuskers* (1918). The foreword to *The People, Yes* promises that the poem will be interspersed

> with interludes of midnight cool blue and inviolable stars over the phantom frames of skyscrapers.

And the skyscraper reappears in the poem as an emblem of the people:

> They have made these steel skeletons like themselves—
> Lean, tumultuous, restless:

21. Carl Sandburg, *Complete Poems* (New York: Harcourt, Brace and Company, 1950), pp. 311, 479, 562.

> *They have put up tall witnesses,*
> *to fade in a cool midnight blue,*
> *to rise in evening rainbow prints.*[22]

The passage brings equally to mind the other mood of the poetry, that in which Sandburg reports the people in their "lean, tumultuous, restless" character, and captures them at their most vigorous and exuberant. The poem "Chicago" is the most familiar and perhaps the starkest instance—and the instance most arresting in its industrial foreground. Or there were the tall yarns that Sandburg related in *The People, Yes*—yarns that disclose the extravagant temper of the people: tales

> *Of a skyscraper so tall they had to put hinges*
> *On the two top stories so to let the moon go by,*
> *Of one corn crop in Missouri when the roots*
> *Went so deep and drew off so much water*
> *The Mississippi riverbed that year was dry. . . .*[23]

Among a people whose every significant gesture is touched with a poetry of immensity, the disciplines of work would reveal no property meticulously separate from the whole. Sandburg's poems create a world of steel and machines and industrial cities, and when the disciplined techniques of our era are mentioned, they appear as tokens of the will and the imaginative power of mankind. The people, Sandburg wrote in *The People, Yes*, is a knower, knowing with an exactness that divides inches into millionths and billionths:

> *Knowing in the mystery of one automatic*
> *machine expertly shaping for your eyes*
> *another automatic machine*

22. *Ibid.*, pp. 437, 598.
23. *Ibid.*, p. 491.

> *Knowing in traction, power-shafts, transmission,*
> *twist drills, grinding, gears—*

and Sandburg described a hard young man whose intellect is shaped for a technological age.

> *Bred in a motorized world of trial and error*
> *He measures by millionths of an inch,*

and his knowledge is of ball bearings, the handling of machine tools, the treatment of steel.[24] Such men, such knowledge, have been for Sandburg the inventive soul of the people embodied for a new era; the technique is absorbed into the energy of the human enterprise.

24. *Ibid.*, pp. 463, 598–599.

# Chapter 6

# Harold Stearns
# and Lewis Mumford

## IN AFFIRMATION OF THE MACHINE

EACH in its own way, the machine societies of Veblen and of Sandburg are hardy and self-sufficient. Yet their self-sufficiency rests upon a power to satisfy separate human needs; their strength is that of assertion and not of inclusion, for neither is expressly a social organism, harmonizing within itself as within a living body all the elements that go to make up and sustain a balanced human experience. In Veblen's civilization of engineers, mankind fulfills its sense of fact rather than its perception of mystery, its appreciation of system rather than its appreciation of freedom and of fresh potentiality, its sober rather than its passionate virtues. Such a civilization would have as its highest goal an evenly distributed material well-being; as its finest morality, a conscientious adherence to mechanical accuracy in labor; as its most humane enjoyments, a dry curiosity in fields of science and learning and an artistic pleasure in the skillful conduct of work. Sandburg's society, on the other hand, is strongest in those areas of human life where Veblen's is weakest. Admittedly, Sandburg's America might be described as an organic society. Its energies are synthesized by its democratic political tradition, and its citizens are a blend of hard technical skill with lusty imagination and homely sensitivity. But Sandburg has not sought to portray the mixtures and careful balances that persist in societies: he tends to select from the whole those activities that represent the less cerebral, the more emotional of human purposes.

With only a moderate shift in emphasis, Veblen's interpretation of the intellect tutored by the machine can be made to describe an intellect capable of positive relationship with the passions and intuitions. The writings of Lewis Mumford and of Harold Stearns describe a machine civilization that has become an organism. Stearns, the young American sophisticate of the nineteen twenties and returned exile of the thirties, stood for the values of urbanity and cultivation, the graces of the liberal mind; and these values, possessing emotional breadth, possess also something of the crystalline polish of the machine. Far more extensively than Stearns—more extensively, perhaps, than any other American author—Mumford has investigated the machine in its social implications; he has found there a discipline worthy of being grafted into a rich cultural tissue.

### HAROLD STEARNS

Editor of *Civilization in the United States* (1922)—a critical commentary upon America outstanding for its day —and expatriate in a period when expatriation was the ultimate symbol of literary dissent, Harold Stearns personified the spiritual revolt among the artists and intellectuals of the days that followed the First World War. Puritanism, industrial regimentation, all the many forces in American life that might make for repression of the human self— these constituted for Stearns as for other rebellious members of his generation the evils that smothered the essential vitality of America. Yet within a few years Stearns was writing with enthusiasm of his rediscovered country, and with admiration for its technologically disciplined mind. During the intervening time there seems to have been no essential change in his own scheme of moral and cultural values; it was the nation that appeared to transform itself before his eyes. Even in his younger days he was calling for a kind of discipline that later he found deeply ingrained in America's business and technological civilization—a discipline that possesses both similarities and contrasts to that which Veblen identified with industrial society.

In fact, a note of austerity runs throughout Stearns's writing. It is present in his *Liberalism in America*, a protest against the war psychology that had settled upon the country by 1917 and against the spirit of conformity. The book was a plea for the maintenance of the liberal outlook, its reasoned and temperate method. Liberalism, Stearns said, "is scientific, curious, experimental"; it does not hide from opposing points of view; it is mellow and unexcited. "It is in a way frankly *au-dessus de la melée*, although not through arrogance but simply from a conviction that liberalism's best service can be performed through creating a certain tolerant temper in society at large." The habits of liberalism are the habits of self-control; in condemning the efforts of the moralists to legislate goodness, Stearns affirmed the superiority of "inner discipline" over "outer compulsion."[1]

1. *Liberalism in America: Its Origin, Its Temporary Collapse, Its Future* (New York: Boni and Liveright, 1919), pp. 27–31, 66–67.

Stearns's main concern was for the free play of the tempered intellect. But he insisted that the mind must root itself in the body and the senses. Attacking the genteel tradition for its fear of vital experience, he argued in "The Intellectual Life"—an article he included in *Civilization in the United States*—that human thought,

> like mist, arises from the earth, and to it must eventually return, if it is not to be dissipated into the ether. The genteel tradition, which has stolen from the intellectual life its own proper possessions, gaiety and laughter, has left it sour and *déraciné.*

Thought must come into some relationship with flesh; true thinkers make no "ascetic divorce between the passions and the intellect, the emotions and the reason." In a soil such as ours, "choked with the feckless weeds of correctness," the mind can find little sustenance.[2]

Stearns would, it seems, make of the trained and disciplined intellect the foundation of a sound culture. But it is an intellect more intuitive, more broadly humane than the industrial mind that Veblen portrayed in his sociological studies. The intelligence to which Stearns referred would occupy a middle ground between the cold and mechanistic world of the pure rationality and the libidinous world of the flesh; it would retain a certain aloofness, would guard itself against uncontrolled passion, yet because of its own maturity and composure it could afford to move freely in the realm of sensuous experience and there seek its nourishment. And its discipline must above all be intelligent and inward—not an external repression dumbly borne by an uncomprehending mind.

2. *Civilization in the United States: An Inquiry by Thirty Americans,* edited by Harold E. Stearns (New York: Harcourt, Brace and Company, 1922), pp. 147–148.

Among the regimentations that would crush the human spirit Stearns placed the regimentation of industrialism, which he glumly analyzed in *America and the Young Intellectual*. "The recent war . . . was in the deepest sense a revolt against the repressions and discipline of an iron industrialism. Human nature simply could not stand the inner strain. . . ." Stearns compared the situation to the disintegration of Sparta, which began almost at the moment that discipline in the ancient city had been brought to its peak. Modern warfare, he warned, would be recurrent if industrialism continued in its existing course.

Man, Stearns argued, is a creature of enormous adaptability and suppleness, and his whole being cries out for a varied experience—for constant change in labor, pace, thought, and surroundings. Where the methods of industrialism hold sway, the varieties of life disappear and a mechanical regularity takes their place. And a way must be found to break this industrial routine.

> After all, a man is much more a playing than a working animal; against his inclinations he can be driven only so far. . . . To procure by drill and regimentation certain habits of regularity and acceptance of industrial routine, is merely transitory and deceptive. Modern industrialism must be made to conform to the true nature of man, and until it has been so made, anything in the shape of true human progress is impossible.[3]

In *Liberalism in America*, however, Stearns suggested that industrial processes might provide a schooling in liberal rationality.[4] He was to make further use of the idea later in his career, when he came to a new appreciation of

3. *America and the Young Intellectual* (New York: George H. Doran Company, 1921), pp. 129–131.
4. *Liberalism in America*, pp. 72–74.

his native land: though he would remain hostile to the factory itself and its own monotonous routines.[5]

Stearns spent most of the period between 1921 and 1932 as an exile in France, doing newspaper work and becoming—so Carl Van Doren informs us—a special legend of the expatriate decade.[6] A combination of personal discouragements drove him back to America. In 1934 appeared his *Rediscovering America*; in 1935, the autobiographical work *The Street I Know*; in 1937, *America: A Re-appraisal*; and in 1938, *America Now*, a new volume of essays on the United States with Stearns as editor and contributor—a work conceived on the plan of *Civilization in the United States*, but distinctly more favorable in its approach.

The mellowed judgments of these later works, the delight in the vigor and the promise of American society, make a sharp contrast to the tone of Stearns's Prohibition-era writings. But the basic preoccupations were unchanged; America was to be tested by the standards of a benign and urbane liberalism. Even in his earlier observations Stearns had been able to find animal vitality and mental keenness in America, and to write:

> We are a land of sunshine and plenty; a land of sparkling, electrical air; a land of many strains of blood, quickly transforming themselves in the amalgam into a type quite distinct from the Anglo-Saxon. . . . Give us half a chance, and we like nothing better than to laugh and play and be gay.[7]

By the slightest shift in emphasis and mood, on the part

5. *The Street I Know* (New York: Lee Furman, 1935), pp. 43–45.

6. *The Nation*, CXLI (November 13, 1935), 574. In a review of *The Street I Know*.

7. *Civilization in the United States*, p. 150; *America and the Young Intellectual*, p. 68.

either of Stearns or the society he observed, this health could be seen to predominate; and in the years that intervened between the *Civilization* and the *Re-appraisal*, both Stearns and his America had matured. The author must have lost much of the natural rebelliousness of youth, and his years of exile could give him time for a fresh perspective, while America grew in cultural sophistication, repealed the *bête noire* of the young postwar intellectuals, Prohibition, and entered into a period of political force and hopefulness. Finally, by the mid-thirties the freedom and sanity of America could be contrasted to the totalitarian menace abroad. Through influences as subtle and yet as telling as these, it would appear, Stearns came to his new appreciation of America.

Of most interest is Stearns's increased recognition of an element in American life to which he had already paid his respects in *Liberalism in America*—the education in rationality given by the technological process. In the *Re-appraisal* he placed much emphasis upon the strength of an American mentality conditioned by technology—but conditioned to intellectual self-discipline, trained to a flexible and imaginative reason of a type that Stearns had always championed. Basing his argument partially upon that of Veblen, he observed that the "discipline of technological facts is constant and unremitting in our life"; we live in the midst of a man-made chemical and mechanical complex, and its workings drill our minds in a grasp of causal sequence, in scientific procedure and the experimental method. America, he said, was engaged in a form of gambling, but gambling of a creative kind—a willingness to experiment and to labor scientifically on the wager that economic and social problems can be solved. It is gambling that "stems from our national discipline—the only valid one we have—of applied science, the discipline that comes from seeing for ourselves how precise knowledge can be made to work."[8]

Stearns did not make Veblen's distinction between the engineer and the businessman. In fact, he pictured the latter as particularly representative of the intelligence of technological and scientific America. Stearns considered modern business to be an intellectually demanding complexity of interrelated parts—where the executive must have knowledge of the skills of secretaries and stenographers along with a knowledge of mathematics and of statistical information, must be aware of economic facts and legal restrictions, and above all must be able to view the future imaginatively. In this form, Stearns maintained, business was taking on the nature of a profession, for which a definite technical education was in order. He detected a reappearance of the prestige once held by the primitive captain of industry.

> It is coming back just in proportion as business is taken, not as an enterprise in buccaneering, but as a discipline—not as an expression of mere energy run wild but also as an occasion for the use of a little thought and intelligent planning.[9]

The businessman as Stearns saw him is a technician—but a technician who combines creative imagination with reasoned technique.

### LEWIS MUMFORD

Possibly no author with the exception of Veblen has written so directly and so extensively of the machine as has Lewis Mumford, and Mumford has contributed to his

---

8. *America: A Re-appraisal* (New York: Hillman-Curl, 1937), pp. 98–99, 288–290.

9. *Ibid.*, pp. 141–144.

studies a humanistic learning and a catholicity of interest that Veblen lacked. The result is a body of writing that leaves untouched almost no phase of the machine as a cultural event: its intellectual and social origins, its history and its evolutions, its relationship to the whole personality. The work of Mumford needs little elucidation, and its themes are too diverse and too elaborately developed to allow of complete summarization. But certain of his theses bear with special force upon the problem of machine discipline and its place in a living social structure.

Mumford is not a student of the machine alone; he is equally known for his architectural criticism, and he has worked in the field of city planning and urban history. These activities have provided context in which to fit the machine; but Mumford's interpretations of architecture, technology, and the city are also subsumed under a more basic preoccupation: his concern for the organic society. His respect for the "functionalist" canon, his belief that the aesthetic form of a useful object should be consistent with the purpose and expressive of it, amounts to a regard for organism. And Mumford displays an equal solicitude for the integrity of the person: wherever contemporary civilization permits either the lapse or the revolt of some human faculty, wherever it fails to hold in unity all elements in the personality, there he has spotted danger. By the same token, of course, a society may be judged whole only if it reflects or supports the wholeness of its persons and is itself organically united to human character.

In Mumford's analysis, the machine bears a paradoxical effect upon personal and social health. As a discipline, it symbolizes and sustains one isolated set of attributes—the least "personal," in fact: the rational, the objective, the detached—and must appear at first sight an enemy to life. Yet in strengthening the objective side of the personality, it enhances some of the finest of human traits, and at the same time it provides a means for repenetration into the dominions of intuition and experience.

### The Machine: Autonomous, and Reconciled

The machine, Mumford has insisted, is the achievement and the symbol of an abstraction. Its coming marked the assertion of one cold element in man's nature, severed from the warm and compounded total; the dissolution of existence into its primary qualities and its abstract time sequences, those bleak and personless dimensions that are grasped by bleak human rationality; and the imposition, upon natural human life-rhythms, of a routine mechanically timed.

First, there is the new conceiving of time. In his superb *Technics and Civilization*, Mumford claimed that the machine was heralded by the ringing of time in the monasteries and in the cities and the development of the clock: here is one of the many ways, he argued, in which the discipline of the monastic orders helped prepare the way for modern mechanical society. The clock is one of the most advanced of machines, a model for others and, in its perfecting, a study in the principles of motion; but in addition, "by its essential nature it dissociated time from human events and helped create the belief in an independent world of mathematically measurable sequences: the special world of science." This world is hardly discoverable in normal experience, where days are uneven, where breathing and pulse vary, where time is measured by events—the lambing of ewes, the time of sowing or of harvest; "if growth has its own duration and regularities, behind it are not simply matter and motion but the facts of development: in short, history." While mechanical time, moreover, is a succession of isolated moments, "organic time" is cumulative.[10] The clock establishes abstract time, and abstract time makes existence intelligible to the mind and purposes of modern science.

Through science, other areas of existence are apprehended in the same calculable terms. The physical sciences rest in part upon

> the elimination of qualities, and the reduction of the complex to the simple by paying attention only to those aspects of events which could be weighed, measured, or counted, and to the particular kind of space-time sequence that could be controlled and repeated—or, as in astronomy, whose repetition could be predicted.

In sum, science has in the past dealt only in the "primary qualities" and abstract physical relationships—mass, motion, and the like—because these conditions seemed most immediately relevant to the objectives of science. And this world-view has given respectability to the machine, for machines have usually been conceived in their primary qualities; they therefore appear to be the most real, the most fitting denizens of a universe that is seen to be, in its essence, pure matter and motion.[11]

Along with the projection of an inorganic, impersonal world, there have come about shifts in the interpretation of human character and new roles for men to fulfill. The investigator is expected to deal with his materials in an entirely objective way. The concentration upon primary qualities "neutralized in experiment and analysis the sensory and emotional reactions of the observer: apart from the process of thinking, he became an instrument of record," and scientific technique became impersonal.

---

10. *Technics and Civilization* (New York: Harcourt, Brace and Company, 1934), pp. 12–18.
11. *Ibid.*, pp. 45–51.

This technique resulted in a valuable moralization of thought: the standards, first worked out in realms foreign to man's personal aims and immediate interests, were equally applicable to more complex aspects of reality that stood closer to his hopes, loves, ambitions.

Less desirable has been the tendency to scorn as unreal the subjective and the intuitive.[12]

The mind is disciplined to objectivity; meanwhile, mind and body are disciplined to abstract time and to the tempo of mechanical civilization, a tempo that takes no account of the organic rhythms and urges. The moment of rising will no longer wait upon strain or fatigue; the hour of eating is not determined by hunger; the working day is marked off by the time clock; play-impulses that pulsate at something other than a mechanical regularity are not integrated into the scheme of events. The real gain in mechanical efficiency is unquestionable; the loss is equally real.[13]

To establish the autonomy of a universe of space-time-mass-motion-number by denying color and scent and life, and the autonomy of the objective reason by denying the emotions, to disrupt the cadences of flesh and mood in favor of mechanical sequence, quite plainly signifies at least the temporary discard of organism. Mumford drew the moral: he pointed to the injuries inflicted upon the human spirit, and in his recent writings he has warned that a self-isolated scientific impersonality and a repression of the subjective life could lead us to nuclear catastrophe. But in *Technics and Civilization*, his greatest condemnation was reserved for "paleotechnic" industry.

The term had been employed by the Scots biologist and sociologist Patrick Geddes to designate the more primitive

12. *Ibid.*, pp. 46, 49, 51.
13. *Ibid.*, pp. 17–18, 269–271.

stage of industrialism, ugly and confused, which was to give way to a refined "neotechnic" stage—Mumford also discovered a third "eotechnic" period at the dawn of modern technology. The paleotechnic methods held sway in the late eighteenth and the nineteenth centuries and still possessed considerable force into the twentieth. At its origins an era of coal and iron, the paleotechnic age was a time of some splendid achievements but also of brutal factory discipline and of social and environmental degradation. In a manner, it represented the machine at its most destructive of life; yet in Mumford's description it did not seem to be the ultimate in mechanical abstraction, for actually its instruments were often cumbersome and inefficient, and frequently it showed little interest in exact scientific knowledge.[14]

Tearing loose from the vital structure of the person, mechanical rationality brings discord to man and to his environment. At the same time, Mumford demonstrated, in winning its independence the rationality has gained something of great value—a chance to cultivate its own latent powers to their fullest so that, returning to its place within the organic personality, it might contribute new strengths to human character; while its twin creations and supports, science and the machine, properly subdued within the social organism might offer fresh possibilities for the enrichment of life. Mumford's view of this reconciliation between vitality and the objective reason can be illustrated by combination of several themes that are separately developed in different parts of his work, and especially in *Technics and Civilization*.

To begin, objective reason *is* an element in the personality, even if it is the most "impersonal" element; its vigor

14. *Ibid.*, pp. 151–211, "The Paleotechnic Phase," *passim*, and pp. 167–168, 194.

should grace the whole man as surely as the vigor of a single limb graces the body. For Mumford, the modern mind possesses the dignity of self-abnegation: trained in detached observation of neutral physical fact, it learns to retain its objectivity even when it deals with matters that come nearer to its own passions and ambitions. A rational detachment is enforced by the machine itself, which can be operated on no other basis; and attending that detachment is "a modulation of emphasis, a matter-of-factness, a reasonableness, a quiet assurance of a neutral realm in which the most obdurate differences can be understood, if not composed."[15]

Here the mechanical intellect has attained a strength in isolation. The wall between intellect and feeling is breached, however, when the modern reason learns to apply the "functionalist" principle to its productions in steel and stone—learns that in building factories that are more simply and perfectly factory-like, and machines that are more rationally machine-like, it achieves a victory not only of efficiency but of aesthetics. Here, of course, is the machine aesthetic of which Sherwood Anderson wrote; in effect, it is rationality sublimated into poetry. As Mumford said in *Sticks and Stones*, "the clean surfaces, the hard lines, the calibrated perfection that the machine has made possible carry with them a beauty quite different from that of handicraft—but often it is a beauty."[16] In *Technics and Civilization* he explained:

> Expression through the machine implies the recognition of relatively new esthetic terms: precision, calculation, flawlessness, simplicity, economy. Feeling attaches itself in these

15. *Ibid.*, pp. 49, 362.
16. *Sticks and Stones: A Study of American Architecture and Civilization* (Second revised edition; New York: Dover Publications, 1955. Originally published in 1924 by Boni and Liveright), p. 178.

new forms to different qualities than those that made handicraft so entertaining. Success here consists in the elimination of the non-essential, rather than, as in handicraft decoration, in the willing production of superfluity, contributed by the worker out of his own delight in the work. The elegance of a mathematical equation, the inevitability of a series of physical inter-relations, the naked quality of the material itself, the tight logic of the whole—these are the ingredients that go into the design of machines: and they go equally into products that have been properly designed for machine production. In handicraft it is the worker who is represented: in machine design it is the work. In handicraft, the personal touch is emphasized, and the imprint of the worker and his tool are both inevitable: in machine work the impersonal prevails, and if the worker leaves any tell-tale evidence of his part in the operation, it is a defect or a flaw.[17]

A more specific aesthetic medium provided by the machine is that of photography. Its value, Mumford argued, is that it aids us in the perception of things on their own terms as they are given form by light and shade and not by the artist's willful fancy. The photographer must respect the essential nature of the object he aims to capture; the challenge is to recognize "the unique esthetic moment" that is worth recording, and precisely to correlate that moment with the tools and conditions of photography.[18] The virtues of the photographer, it would appear, are in essence those of the scientist: objectivity, submission to fact, an unobtrusiveness of the self.

The aesthetic of the machine is especially the achievement of the period that Geddes and Mumford have called "neotechnic"—the age that is supplanting iron and confusion with electricity and chemicals, with light metals, with methods informed by science and far more carefully

17. *Technics and Civilization*, pp. 350–351.
18. *Ibid.*, pp. 337–341.

devised than those of the paleotechnic past. And besides the beauty that the neotechnic mind brings to the machine and the environment, the same mind makes an even more significant incursion into the areas of existence originally shunned by the machine: it turns to the study of biology, organism, human life and society. Through the new interest and new investigation, Mumford claimed, the machine and the machine intellect have themselves undergone a transformation. Thought no longer holds exclusively to the inanimate dimensions and measurements of matter; there is a growing consciousness of organic forms and adaptations, and this consciousness has aided in the sophistication of technics—as the shapes of fish and of turtles have taught lessons in efficient form.[19]

Finally, Mumford believed, in many ways the neotechnic machine has made possible a social ordering fitted to a harmonious existence for men. In his latest writing, to be sure, he has spoken gloomily of the advent of the megalopolis, the giant sprawling city that would lose all contact with the land; but in *Technics and Civilization*, he maintained that the increasing industrialization of agriculture and the tightening relationship between the agrarian and the machine economies might modify the character of both and bring them into closer unity.[20] Mumford found, moreover, that the neotechnic era was preparing the demise of factory slavery; the new techniques were reducing the relative number of routine factory jobs of the old type and changing the nature of machine tending itself.

> The qualities the new worker needs are alertness, responsiveness, an intelligent grasp of the operative parts: in short, he

19. *Ibid.*, pp. 216–217, 250–255.
20. *Ibid.*, p. 259. For a more pessimistic outlook, see *The City in History: Its Origins, Its Transformations, and Its Prospects* (New York: Harcourt, Brace and World, 1961), *passim.*

must be an all-round mechanic rather than a specialized hand.... [W]ith complete automatism freedom of movement and initiative return for that small part of the original working force now needed to operate the plant.[21]

It may be noted that in much of what they had to say, Mumford and Sherwood Anderson revealed a strikingly similar awareness of the contrast between twentieth-century industrialism and that which preceded it and of the special properties, technical and aesthetic, of the more recent industry. Yet, where Anderson detected an intensified routinization of factory labor, Mumford discovered liberation.

The modern intelligence, as Mumford viewed it in *Technics and Civilization*, is disciplined in the exact methods that Veblen described. But the discipline will not of necessity produce the race of single-minded, factual technicians of whom Veblen spoke; it may provide avenues into varied realms of feeling and imagining and do its part in the formation of a personality and a culture that are whole within themselves and organic to each other. And while Veblen was most concerned with the education in logic and in technical facility that is furnished by the machine, Mumford dealt with an education more distinctly moral—a discipline in intellectual detachment which includes a detachment from personal whim and passion. Originally the product of objective reason, the machine independently imposes the objective standard upon human thought and behavior.[22]

*Nuclear Armament*

In *Technics and Civilization*, Mumford arrived at his most favorable appraisal of the machine. With the passage

21. *Technics and Civilization*, pp. 224–229.
22. *Ibid.*, pp. 324, 362.

of time, he has apparently found increased cause for apprehension over the trend of machine society.

From America's participation in the First World War, John Dos Passos drew some of his first lessons in the nature of social regimentation. Harold Stearns examined the conduct of an industrial nation as it broke, so he claimed, from the repressions of the machine into the ferocity of warfare. Among other authors of the Lost Generation, the experience of war could deepen cynicism and awaken angers to be unleashed more comprehensively against the social environment. But after the totalitarian aggressions of the late nineteen thirties, after Hiroshima and the lengthening of the Cold War, the idea that militarism is an ultimate form of the machine could take on a fresh plausibility. To that idea Lewis Mumford has given particularly eloquent utterance. Even in *The Story of Utopias* and *Technics and Civilization,* he had written of the alliances of warfare with science or the machine.[23] Then, as international crisis deepened, he began to project the theme of militarism more centrally into his study of the machine and contemporary civilization. In *Men Must Act* (1939) and *Faith for Living* (1940), he sought to alert the American public to the fascist threat in Europe; more lately, he has denounced the nuclear armaments of the Eastern and Western blocs.

Mumford describes a dual process by which the modern era sets the conditions for disaster. On the one hand, through its unbending routines and its overconcentration upon the rational, it reduces to barbarism the deeper, the emotional and instinctive, ingredient of the personality. Neglected, given no coherent education that would order its drives and awaken its higher potentialities, that ingre-

23. *The Story of Utopias* (New York: Boni and Liveright, 1922), pp. 276–277; *Technics and Civilization,* pp. 81–96, 307–311.

dient—which might otherwise assert some human dominance over the machine—atrophies or else drifts into savagery; in fact, it explodes in nihilistic revolt as it frets against the sterilities of its surroundings.[24] And while science and machinery produce the barbarian, they produce the passive servant of the fascist or militarist state. The masses are so conditioned to routine and to external stimuli that they become the inert instruments of totalitarianism; the scientist, through a misuse of the objectivity that is his very real virtue, detaches himself from responsibility for his acts, and compulsively pursues knowledge and sources of power without thought to the ends to be served.[25] Together, "the automaton and the id"[26]— the latter encouraged in its anarchy by a distortion of Freudianism and by tendencies within the romantic tradition—threaten calamity.

One is reluctant to leave the problem precisely as Mumford has left it; his own treatment opens lines of speculation that he has almost but not quite traced to their finish. Placing the blame for nuclear armament upon the modern spirit, he has made little effort to evaluate the relative part played by the peculiar dilemmas of international politics,

24. *Men Must Act* (New York: Harcourt, Brace and Company, 1939), p. 27; *Faith for Living* (New York: Harcourt, Brace and Company, 1940), pp. 36–37; *Values for Survival: Essays, Addresses, and Letters on Politics and Education* (New York: Harcourt, Brace and Company, 1946), pp. 180–181, 203; *The Conduct of Life* (New York: Harcourt, Brace and Company, 1951), p. 16; *Art and Technics* (New York: Columbia University Press, 1952), pp. 10–15, 152, 158–159.

25. *The Conduct of Life*, pp. 14–17; *In the Name of Sanity* (New York: Harcourt, Brace and Company, 1954), pp. 194–199; *The City in History*, p. 4.

26. *In the Name of Sanity*, p. 199. Much of the chapter "The Uprising of Caliban," pp. 166–203, is devoted to criticism of the modern philosophies that preach unlimited expression of the feelings.

or simply by the circumstance that the production of a nuclear weapon is now physically possible; he has implicitly assumed that another age, possessed of the ability to make an atomic bomb, would have refrained. He has also failed to give attention to certain phenomena of our era that are as notable as nuclear power itself: the intricate controls, moral and administrative, that have been thrown around it, and the remarkable absence both of panic and of xenophobia among the populations that must live with it—compare the semiracist hatreds against the Germans in 1918 with the attitude today toward the Soviet, and reciprocally toward the American, populations.

These are the obvious qualifications that could be brought to bear upon Mumford's argument; an equally significant qualification might be evolved from some of Mumford's own insights. For surely the disciplined mind that he described in *Technics and Civilization,* or the tough and supple intelligence that could survive within Thorstein Veblen's exacting industrial world, would be trained in many of the virtues especially required for the mastery of atomic power: a tempered detachment with which to subdue the primitive impulses within the self, a hardened nerve with which to confront the complex dangers of a thermonuclear environment, and a technical genius with which to command the elaborate mechanical and social structures of the atomic age. And if some of the skilled restraints that governments and peoples have demonstrated in nuclear politics are more directly attributable to the threat itself, then the atom has become, like its scientific and mechanical antecedents, an influence for technical skill and emotional restraint. In *Technics and Civilization,* Mumford specifically represented the self-control, the objective reasonableness of the modern character as a contrast to political barbarism, and he has never lost sight of the fine strengths in the modern intellect;[27] had he continued to emphasize their full possibilities, he might have granted them a greater role in the building of a stable peace.

27. *Technics and Civilization*, pp. 362–363; *Faith for Living*, pp. 93–94; *Values for Survival*, p. 124; *The Conduct of Life*, pp. 18, 83; *Art and Technics*, pp. 40–54; *The City in History*, p. 366.

# Chapter 7

# Sinclair Lewis

## IN AFFIRMATION OF MAIN STREET

AN exactness in detail, coupled with an openness— almost a deliberate inconclusiveness—in final statement and appraisal, is characteristic of the novels of Sinclair Lewis. He could report the moments of an ordinary day with so careful an attention to its most minute and typical incident that the reader is actually startled at the unexpected familiarity, the strong circumstantiality;[1] and each incident, in itself, may call forth from author and reader at least implicit moral judgment. But precisely because the itemization is so thorough, ultimate judgment is held in suspension. Fact is set against fact, valuation

---

1. Alfred Kazin referred to Lewis's "photographic exactness," and said that Lewis "dramatized the new realism by making the novel an exact and mimetic transcription of American life. . . ." *On Native Grounds*, pp. 208, 210.

against valuation: Babbitt's vulgarity, his pathos; Max Gottlieb's splendidly rigorous science, his paralyzing aloofness. Possibly the best example is *Dodsworth*, in which Lewis maintained a steady tension between the values of Europe and those of America. It may be that none of Lewis's other work established so careful a balance as that in *Dodsworth*; certainly, each novel has some predominant bent, some argument that the author allowed to prevail over its antagonist, and occasionally, as in *Elmer Gantry*, the satire becomes bluntly weighted. But even in *Main Street* or *Babbitt*, Lewis never permitted his reader to lose sight of the virtues that lay in those features of American life he attacked. And the balance that is sustained within individual novels subsists even more firmly through Lewis's work as a whole—*Arrowsmith* against *Work of Art*, or *Babbitt* against *The Prodigal Parents* against *Kingsblood Royal*.

Lewis was on particularly intimate terms with his America, and from this intimacy, perhaps, his thinking drew some of its flexibility. Mark Schorer in his exhaustive biography and Alfred Kazin in *On Native Grounds* have stressed the depth of Lewis's rooting in the American soil, the essential benevolence of his role as critic. Lewis was so steeped in the culture of middle-class America that his books are as pervaded with a sheer feeling of that culture as with analytical observation about it. The disciplined— or slipshod—American business temper was for Lewis simply a given fact, a part of the American spirit, a thing to be praised, bemoaned, chided, and ultimately accepted for what it is because it is American; and for the most part it was with the business rather than the specifically industrial temper of America that he was concerned.

Lewis's interpretation of America's middle-class disciplines, therefore, does not lend itself to concise summary.

He can be said to have had an impression—or rather, a range of impressions—of those disciplines, but these do not stand separate from the rest of the things the author had to say about his land. His work does, however, divide itself roughly into several periods, and in each period Lewis made some particular evaluation of the American bourgeoisie, with its peculiar disciplines and its tendencies toward mental sloth, its confinements and its dawnings of imagination.

## The Novels of Romance

Between 1912 and 1919, Lewis published a series of novels and short stories with titles that few readers today would recognize. In 1912, under the pseudonym "Tom Graham," he brought out a light, boys' adventure book that has long since been forgotten—*Hike and the Aeroplane*; in 1914 appeared *Our Mr. Wrenn*, the tale of a clerkish adventurer; the following year a story of aviation, *The Trail of the Hawk*; in 1917 *The Job*, with an office girl as heroine, and *The Innocents*, telling of two elderly lovers; and finally, in 1919 *Free Air*, which revealed a romanticism of the automobile and the highway as Lewis had previously romanticized the airplane. These works are joined in an external unity—if only because they all preceded *Main Street*. But there is also a recurrent theme and motif—a romantic theme of love and of adventure, often rather simple in its development. Against the motif of romance Lewis played the office and its sober or stultifying routines.

*Our Mr. Wrenn* concerns the timid little employee of a souvenir company, poised between desire for excitement and an ingrained habit of caution and steadiness. In this novel, the middle-class virtues attain at least a partial moral victory. Lewis did not fail to present the limitations that surrounded the life to which his hero is fitted. When Mr. Wrenn is pictured taking a browbeating from his chief or his landlady, the reader is made conscious of the pathos attending the little man's meek existence. After an ocean voyage, some adventures in England, and a flirtation with a very modern woman, Mr. Wrenn settles down with a job and a wife; and there is the hint that in retaining solidity, the clerk has lost something else.

> Across the ragged vacant lots to the west a vast sunset processional marched down the sky. . . . "Gee!" he mourned, "it's the first time I've noticed a sunset for a month! I used to see knights' flags and Mandalay and all sorts of stuff in sunsets!"

But in place of "his lost kingdom," Mr. Wrenn has the plainer comforts and joys of an evening with his wife.[2]

Even the romance, however, does not seem a contradiction of the rest in Mr. Wrenn's character. For that romance is the expression of a decent and innocent, and therefore a trustfully dreaming mind; also a mind preserved—by workaday, quite inhibiting conditions—from a too-full, a jaded and disillusioned, experience of life. The Wrennish virtues are shown off to best advantage when they are contrasted to the shallowness of the aesthetes the hero confronts in England—particularly Mr. Wrenn's heroine Istra Nash, impulsive, devoid of self-restraint, lost and miserable in her awareness of being lost. And in the face of a snickering sophistication, meek bourgeois moralism can even expand into militancy.[3]

In sum, the middle-class conventionalities and self-restrictions and timidities that appear to stand between Mr. Wrenn and the fulfillment of his deepest urges might be considered the most wholesome of disciplines. Not the lean

2. *Our Mr. Wrenn: The Romantic Adventures of a Gentle Man* (New York and London: Harper and Brothers, 1914), p. 254.

3. *Ibid.*, pp. 136–137.

hard discipline of Anderson's *Poor White* or Veblen's technicians: something more shyly warm, more contented and
domestic; but discipline of a kind, nevertheless, preserving
the decencies in Mr. Wrenn's character even in confining
it.

*Our Mr. Wrenn*, however, does not give quite the sense
we want to consider. Even to describe as a discipline the
Wrennish way of life is possibly to take liberties with the
story. Little Mr. Wrenn does not simply withdraw, severely
and frigidly, from experience; more accurately, he is not
so constituted as to be able to participate in it. The business temperament of which Lewis wrote in *Dodsworth* and
elsewhere is of sterner quality than this.

In *The Trail of the Hawk*, business and adventure come
again into conflict. In the final pages of the novel, Lewis
had his aviator hero, Carl Ericson, triumph over a temporary subservience to office drudgery that might have stifled
the free soul in him. And in *The Job*—perhaps the least
romantic of the early novels—Lewis brought an even closer
criticism to bear upon the office. The heroine, Una Golden,
does forge for herself a business career. But her struggle
seems almost to be against, rather than within, the office—
a resistance to a monotony, to a pressure of time, to an existence occupied with inanimate things and sealed off from
life and warmth: to all those forces that would consume
her vitality. The "savage continuity" of office work, sustained because each worker is part of a closely fitted structure and cannot establish his own rhythm of labor without
breaking that of the whole; the "airless, unnatural, strain-
ing life" that exhausts and brings a mood of worry: all this
amounts to a fairly typical kind of literary indictment.
Lewis found in modern business a nobility that proceeds
from its gradually expanding vision and its progress toward

efficiency;[4] but these qualities are not synonymous with business as a form of work.

"Moths in the Arc Light," a short piece of 1919, bears a similar message. It is the story of a man and woman whose love is a victory of living humanity over the deadness of the office. But here Lewis was responsive to some of the hard values of the business world. The main character, Bates, is pictured as a businessman of the new generation, neat, polished: "yet in decision he was firm as a chunk of flint." Lewis said of an office building:

> It had the charm of efficiency that is beginning to make American cities beautiful with a beauty that borrows nothing from French châteaux or English inns. The architect . . . had created a building as clean and straight and honest as the blade of a sword. It made Bates glad that he was a business man.[5]

The point is echoed in the first words of *Babbitt*:

> The towers of Zenith aspired above the morning mist; austere towers of steel and cement and limestone, sturdy as cliffs and delicate as silver rods. They were neither citadels nor churches, but frankly and beautifully office-buildings.[6]

## The Novels of Dissent

From the appearance of *Main Street*, in 1920, to the publication in 1928 of *The Man Who Knew Coolidge*, Lewis was doing the work that won him his fame as a satirist of the American bourgeoisie. During these years Lewis estab-

---

4. *The Job: An American Novel* (New York and London: Harper and Brothers, 1917), pp. 25–26, 44, 162.

5. *Selected Short Stories of Sinclair Lewis* (Garden City, N. Y.: Doubleday, Doran and Company, 1935), pp. 342, 344.

6. *Babbitt* (New York: Harcourt, Brace and Company, 1922), p. 1.

lished, far more clearly than in his earlier novels, the standards by which he would judge American society; and though later his judgment mellowed, the criteria themselves appear to have remained roughly consistent. For an appreciation of these standards and of their relationship to a concept of discipline, *Arrowsmith* is especially relevant, although the book, published in 1925, is neither the first nor the best known of Lewis's most important volumes.

In a sense, it must be acknowledged, *Arrowsmith* stands apart from the bulk of Lewis's work. It is the only one of the novels in which the heroes deal in the more abstract reaches of higher science. Its major characters are more aloof, in labor, in intellectual temper, and in aim, from American civilization than are those of any other Lewis novel.[7] At the opening of the story, a kinship is suggested between the searching mind of Martin Arrowsmith and the wanderings of a pioneer ancestor. But with modern America Arrowsmith can have no real communication: every attempt on his part, however well intentioned, to adapt himself to his American environment is represented as a betrayal of his mistress, Science.

This conception of science as a thing to itself, a seeking and a method that exist on their own rigorous and ultimate terms, suggests the hard intellectuality that Veblen assigned to the modern world and the clean modern aesthetic that Lewis Mumford has reported in *Technics and Civili-*

---

7. In "Martin Arrowsmith: The Scientist as Hero," Charles E. Rosenberg discussed Lewis's effort, through *Arrowsmith*, to arrive at a definition of a modern heroism; such stature, Lewis believed at the time, could be attained only through a detachment from all the pressures and commercial standards of American life, and science offered a means to this pure detachment. Rosenberg also distinguished between the mechanistic science to which the characters of *Arrowsmith* give their allegiance and the vitalistic science that has done continual intellectual battle with the science of mechanism. *American Quarterly*, XV (Fall 1963), 447–458.

*zation* and Sherwood Anderson in *Perhaps Women.* Like Veblen's scholars, Martin Arrowsmith and his mentor Max Gottlieb demand the right to an idle curiosity and to a pursuit of knowledge unencumbered by commercial or even humanitarian objectives, and Gottlieb wages quite a Veblenian war against university administration. The chaste aesthetic, the austere intellect of Anderson's and Veblen's twentieth-century civilization are called to mind again and again as the novel emphasizes the twin precisions of scientific labor: exactness in analysis, fineness in technique.

Gottlieb possesses a "flair of technique," a "sure rapidity which dignified the slightest movement of his hands"; and, executing some minute and subsidiary task, he lectures his students: " '. . . technique, gentlemen, is the beginning of all science.' " Gottlieb, we are told, has not published heavily, but his papers "were all exquisitely finished, all easily reduplicated and checked by the doubtfulest critics." He rejoices in "the exasperated carefulness" of Arrowsmith's investigations. Martin himself, in his maturity as a scientist,

> desired a perfection of technique in the quest for absolute and provable fact; he desired as greatly as any Pater to "burn with a hard gem-like flame," and he desired not to have ease and repute in the market-place, but rather to keep free of those follies, lest they confuse him and make him soft.[8]

But while Sinclair Lewis created a scientific realm that would square in many respects with the findings of Veblen and others, that realm comes closer to Veblen's community of scholars than to his broader civilization of machines and engineers. Gottlieb and Arrowsmith are most clearly not

8. *Arrowsmith* (New York and Chicago: Harcourt, Brace and Company, 1945), pp. 35–36, 128, 130, 420. Originally published in 1925.

technicians, with a technician's concern for means and uses; these are the concerns of a physician, and Lewis was quite explicit in separating the work of the doctor from that of the scientist. As a physician, entangled in the practical urgencies of his profession and the compromises of commercial America, Arrowsmith almost loses himself; he regains his true direction only when he is sheltered within a research institute that is comparatively, though not absolutely, removed from utilitarian or commercial objectives.

Another distinction is even more telling. The machine, our other authors have insisted, is above all a dictator of pace; and the scientists of *Arrowsmith* seek a liberation from pace, the freedom to do slowly and speculatively the work that can be neither hastened nor timed. The labor of Lewis's scientist heroes is all founded in a careful patience, which is enjoined when Gottlieb advises his students to read Pater's *Marius the Epicurean*, that they might gain from it " 'the calmness which is the secret of laboratory skill' "; or when he says of Americans that they are " 'impatient with the beautiful dullness of long labors' "; or when Arrowsmith prays for " 'unclouded eyes and freedom from haste,' " and the persistence to check through and destroy his own errors.[9] If there is a similarity in structure between the quiet domain in which Arrowsmith moves and the machine-paced world of which Veblen wrote, it would be that the pace of Veblen's industrial society is an element in its complexity and in its exact synchronization of parts, and needs to be grasped with a precision as fine as that with which Arrowsmith analyzes the elements of his microscopic universe.

Yet however distinct Martin Arrowsmith and his fellow laborers may be from the homely middle-class Americans

9. *Ibid.*, pp. 37, 40, 292.

who people most of the Lewis novels, the values to which, in *Arrowsmith*, Lewis gave his assent seem to be in essence those that he would instinctively employ time and again in criticism or in praise of the American bourgeoisie—and throughout *Arrowsmith* these values are expressed with special clarity. For the strongest characters in Lewis's books, the Sam Dodsworths, possess a certain earthy solid competence, a clear-headedness about their job or their politics and a capacity for direct self-examination and self-confrontation; the weakest characters are incompetent and wordy. And how could the most flaccid qualities in American society be more distinctly identified than by their contrast to the craft of scientist as Lewis pictured it?

Here is work that can tolerate no incompetence, that calls for constant re-examination of its own findings, and that cannot cover up even its most minute imperfections by a well-chosen phrase. Measured against its purity, all men who are inexact or self-seeking or even decently mediocre stand sharply exposed: mercenary and social-climbing physicians, medical students who prefer rule-of-thumb to the rigors of accurate knowledge, imprecise and talkative uplifters. *Arrowsmith* therefore provides an even clearer statement than *Babbitt* of the case against Babbittry.

To be sure, the most admirable figures in Lewis's other stories possess an ability of another sort than that of a Gottlieb or an Arrowsmith: theirs is more a matter of good common sense—an intuitive rather than intellectual capability for life and work. But they are like Arrowsmith in their honest skill. Because he is a good workman, Doctor Kennicott manages to achieve, through all his dullness and ignorance, a partial dignity. " 'He speaks a vulgar, common, incorrect German of life and death and birth and the soil,'" marvels Carol—she is accompanying the doctor on an emergency call at a German-American household. " 'I read the French and German of sentimental lovers and Christmas garlands. And I thought that it was I who had the culture!' . . ."[10]

Babbitt, on the other hand, is a bad workman. We are informed that in most matters of real importance to the profession of realtor—architecture, landscape gardening, sanitation, economics, conditions in Zenith—his information is either rudimentary or nonexistent, his conception of his calling limited to its financial return.[11] And this can almost be taken as the central truth about Babbitt, for it epitomizes his wordy and altogether ineffective relationship toward life and his lack of contact with reality. His existence is reproached, not for the tightness of its routinized disciplines, as in *The Job*, but for its slackness. When at the conclusion of the tale Babbitt attains his moment of strength, he appears to be for the first time in full mental command of a thing: he has recognized the concreteness of his son's marriage and ambitions for a technical career, has grasped and championed a fact. It is a rebellion against Babbittry far deeper than Babbitt's earlier fling at flirtation and radicalism, for that episode had been, Booster-like, a matter of fantasies and words. At the same time, Lewis reveals in the final scene something of kindness toward the antic gestures of Booster culture; that way of life, we recognize, represents a romantic quest gone astray, and Babbitt is determined that despite the shocked carpings of family, the son will bring a quest to fulfillment.

## The Novels of Acceptance

The stubborn and disciplined brain of Max Gottlieb might serve as a standard against which to gauge the

10. *Main Street: The Story of Carol Kennicott* (New York: Harcourt, Brace and Howe, 1920), p. 192.

11. *Babbitt*, pp. 42–50.

weakest elements in American life as Lewis depicted them in his fiction of the nineteen twenties: the ignorance of *Main Street's* Gopher Prairie; the verbose inadequacy of Babbitt, or of Lowell Schmaltz in *The Man Who Knew Coolidge*; the careless and half-formed religious idealism upon which Elmer Gantry could prey. Yet a stubbornly disciplined intelligence, Lewis found, is itself native to the American middle class at its best—his portrayal of Kennicott is an illustration—and his later stories proclaim the mental and moral toughness, the plain good workmanship of our bourgeoisie. Moreover, these stories rest their case upon the existence of just that complex of virtues essentially "Puritan" which in the view of so many of Lewis's contemporaries represented the essence and the malady of bourgeois America.

The pivotal novel, of course, is *Dodsworth*. Published in 1929, it was anticipated to an extent in some of Lewis's earlier writing, where a knowing and salty entrepreneur occasionally makes an appearance. Percy Bresnahan of *Main Street* might be an example, though he is full of bluster; and in the second of three articles upon the presidential campaign of 1924—which Lewis ran in fictional form under the title "Be Brisk With Babbitt"—the author had Charles McKelvey, the wealthy contractor of *Babbitt*, desert the entrepreneurial ranks and come out for La Follette, for reasons that disclose a leathery common sense and a liberal spirit.[12] But in *Dodsworth*, Lewis became far more explicit.

Of all the major works of Lewis, *Dodsworth* was the most balanced in its examination of American business. It would seem that the criticisms of the American character that appear in the story possess a shade more force than the defense. But whatever the final verdict, the novel defines

12. *The Nation*, CXIX (October 22, 1924), 437–439.

the sober business spirit as earnestly, essentially American, revealing itself in the very earnest and very American person of Sam Dodsworth, automobile manufacturer. In Lewis's appealing presentation of this man lies at least a partial affirmation of stolid entrepreneurial purposefulness.

Dodsworth is not in all ways the average American. He is an independent industrialist who recoils at the prospect of becoming the creature of an organization; he is a maker of automobiles who can consider himself brother to the "anonymous and merry and vulgar artisans" who had fashioned Notre Dame: his existence essentially defies Veblen's dualism that pits business against the technological spirit. "He was not a Babbitt, not a Rotarian, not an Elk, not a deacon. . . . While he was bored by free verse and cubism, he thought rather well of Dreiser, Cabell, and so much of Proust as he had rather laboriously mastered."[13] Dodsworth, then, represents the businessman at his finest rather than at his average stage of development. But if he brings into the business world attributes of intelligence and sensitivity that are his own, he shares also in the plain qualities that might be expected of the best American industrial leaders. "He was common sense apotheosized, he had the energy and reliability of a dynamo. . . ." Lewis described him tying his tie, "not swiftly but with the unwasteful and extremely unadventurous precision of a man who has introduced as much 'scientific efficiency' into daily domesticity as into his factory."[14]

Honest, stalwart, and rather lumbering, Sam Dodsworth embodies the single-minded drive of American business and at the same time stands above the hysteria to which,

13. *Dodsworth* (New York: Harcourt, Brace and Company, 1929), pp. 11, 16, 141.
14. *Ibid.*, pp. 10–11.

in weaker or less wise men, American hustle tends. Lewis's hero shows to good advantage when he is set beside his wife, a woman of frail and selfish nature whose desire is to dissociate herself from her crude homeland and take on the elegance of what she thinks to be European culture. All through the novel this solid man plods along, tasting the new truths he discovers in Europe, recognizing, slowly and even painfully, the case for the Old World as against the New, and yet never divesting himself of his bulky honesty, never succumbing to the superficial (not the true) Europe that absorbs his wife and that finally impels her to leave him.[15]

In *Dodsworth*, Lewis balanced the strengths and weaknesses of the entrepreneur. In *Work of Art* (1934), he dealt only with the strengths; for he told of Myron Weagle, a hotel keeper who transforms his most prosaic of businesses into an act of creation. Like Martin Arrowsmith or the actress heroine of *Bethel Merriday*, Myron devotes a young lifetime to the mastery of a craft. And as in *Arrowsmith*, Lewis set the sober demands of his hero's calling against some slacker and superficially more promising mode of existence—here represented by Myron's brother, Ora, whose expressed ambition is Art. As the novel progresses, Ora is seen to be without moral substance, and therefore without the integrity or purpose by which his artistic inclinations might be brought to fruition, while Myron, by the force of a persistence wholly Puritanical and bourgeois, struggles to carry the art of hotel management to its perfection.

If the details of conventions or taxation seem to have nothing to do with the soul of Myron Weagle, poet, then is the seem-

15. Although in *World So Wide* (1951), Dodsworth reappears as a permanent resident of Europe.

ing wrong, for it was with such details that he had to harass himself, it was for them that he had to give up leisure and love and play. . . .[16]

*The Prodigal Parents*, which appeared in 1938, gives the proper concluding note. Here the author is settled comfortably with the American middle class he had lauded and chastised in many previous works. Except for the differences in temperament between Fred Cornplow and the meeker hero of *Our Mr. Wrenn*, the novel almost brings the reader full circle to the earlier work; both were written in a similarly pleasant, unargumentative tone. It is not that the American character goes unquestioned. As in *Dodsworth*, there is a conflict, in this case between the routine of Fred Cornplow's life as an automobile dealer and his impulsive effort to break out and travel—much the same battle as that which had been fought within Mr. Wrenn. But the urgency of debate that is to be found in *Dodsworth* is absent. Fred is shrewd and even-tempered as Babbitt was not, and far more realistic than Mr. Wrenn; he is plainly a tower of strength in relation to his soft children; it is equally evident that his kind of strength accompanies the loss of a larger experience of life. There is no question of the respective virtues that lie with either form of living; and to the query, Which should the hero choose?, the novel gives the most obvious and unrevolutionary of answers: He should combine something of each.

Lewis's ultimate appraisal of Fred Cornplow was in essence his continuing appraisal of the Mr. Wrenns and Dr. Kennicotts, the Myron Weagles and Sam Dodsworths he had scrutinized from a hundred standpoints in the course of his literary career. Lewis found Fred Cornplow to be, simply, the indispensable, "eternal bourgeois."

16. *Work of Art* (Garden City, N. Y.: Doubleday, Doran and Company, 1934), p. 267.

He has, at times, been too noisy or too prosy; he has now and then thought more of money than of virtue and music; but he has been the eternal doer; equally depended upon—and equally hated—by the savage mob and by the insolent nobility.

As an Egyptian, Fred Cornplow "planned the pyramids, conciliated the mad pharaohs, tried to make existence endurable for the sweating slaves"; when a Roman, he conquered and helped to rule with a measure of justice the dominions of Rome; his work as an abbot in the Dark Ages was in the development of agriculture and building stone; he served under Cromwell; fought the American Civil War for both sides; and after, "created bribery and railroads" and gave the proceeds to science. He has possessed the name Babbitt, and the name Ben Franklin; and once, in Eugene O'Neill's interpretation, he was called Marco Polo and brought to Europe the exotic Orient.

> He is the eternal bourgeois, the bourjoyce, the burgher, the Middle Class, whom the Bolsheviks hate and imitate, whom the English love and deprecate, and who is most of the population worth considering in France and Germany and these United States.[17]

With the business figures of Anderson's novels, he is forced to narrow patterns of conduct; but with the scientist Arrowsmith, he is the good workman, and in labor his life is vindicated.

17. *The Prodigal Parents* (Garden City, N. Y.: Doubleday, Doran and Company, 1938), pp. 99–100.

# Epilogue

THE twentieth-century literary and aesthetic experience of the machine has defined in industrialism a number of attributes that resolve themselves into polar clusters: bulk, profusion, variegation against exactness, refinement, and form. But these qualities lend themselves to infinite division and combination, and indeed the industrial world of recent American literature is unitary at the same time that it is polar. The pace of the machine may discipline when it is at its most frenetic, and a technological complexity may present itself to the imagination as a massive brokenness, even while its intricate configurations confront and strain the intellect.

If we have encountered a dominant attitude toward the machine and its disciplines, it is one of repudiation. Yet the judgment that the writers offered cannot be considered apart from a dilemma that reaches far beyond the question of mechanism itself and touches upon every reasonably civilized environment. Should that environment primarily be expressive of intuition, an artist's medium for the sensibilities—the Paris of *Three Soldiers,* perhaps; or should it be essentially a lawgiver, resisting and toughening to some specific rule the anarchic materials of human temper—and is submission to arbitrary law not itself a more subtle expression of will and intelligence? This is not to say that the authors rejected discipline when they chose the first of these alternatives. In many respects, they endorsed the highest categories of control—personal, social, and artistic —and Waldo Frank discovered that the decay of cultural form was the sickness of his age; yet their disciplines would be pliant to spontaneous life. And for reasons that the writings themselves have made abundantly clear, the machine is the most logical of symbols for the fact of Law; it stands in conflict with a range of impulses, and its imagery of discipline is perfect.

The discipline may be of varying kinds. It may impose a monotony, as in the case of the simplest factory tasks, or an exacting complexity; again, it may impose an order, whether simple or complex, that constrains the play of feeling, or a disorder that contends against the instinct of continuity—and presumably the complexities of the machine environment verge upon disorder until comprehended and given system. The discipline, moreover, may be in concordance with a modern temperament fully subdued to its routine or quickened and skilled in response to its complications—or in some posture more violent toward fractured or resistant personality. In any event, the discipline exists in a state of tension with its human object, a tension effecting either a clash or an arrangement and disposition of stresses. The material world that once, in some measure, lay passive to the craftsman's touch has sprung to an aggressive life of its own, in an activity incessantly altering and increasingly intricate; it therefore makes necessary an exact human strategy of adjustment and defense—the more so, since every new stratagem will itself become an addition to the technological intricacy that is to be mastered.

But to the degree that the machine lacks the values of impulse and free expression it gains in an antithetic value. For if spontaneity makes its demand upon us, we have also a sense of the ascetic, the rigors of Law; and here the literature of protest does the machine an unconscious honor— at times not quite unconscious. The protest isolates the discipline of the machine as a clearly definable phenomenon and sets it forth in its most imposing symbolism. And when to the hostile critiques are added the more balanced or the favorable analyses provided by Veblen or Mumford, the citizen of the machine era is revealed in his dignity and his unpretentious strength—his technical proficiency, his determination and his self-conquest. We learn also that even in its discipline the machine is capable of an extensive commerce with sensibility: Harold Stearns found that the discipline may be a conditioning in liberal perception; Mumford, that in the most advanced technology it allies itself with organism; Veblen, that it satisfies the instinct of workmanship; Anderson, that for the technician it is the method of art.

The energies of machine society can answer to a need of another sort. It is a need to experience an environment that is more than an ordered rationality: surroundings concrete and substantial, fleshed with a varied detail that may fully engage the senses. The effect is given in a scene from *Manhattan Transfer*:

> Dusk gently smooths crispangled streets. Dark presses tight the steaming asphalt city, crushes the fretwork of windows and lettered signs and chimneys and watertanks and ventilators and fireescapes and moldings and patterns and corrugations and eyes and hands and neckties into blue chunks, into black enormous blocks. Under the rolling heavier heavier pressure windows blurt light. Night crushes bright milk out of arclights, squeezes the sullen blocks until they drip red, yellow, green into streets resounding with feet. All the asphalt oozes light. Light spurts from lettering on roofs, mills dizzily among wheels, stains rolling tons of sky.[1]

The city is at once an anarchic profusion of particulars and a compressed solidity: it has the multiformity and the composition of a highly concrete thing. Machine civilization, in its energies, regains the thickness of which the austerities and abstractions of mechanical technique would strip it.

1. *Manhattan Transfer* (New York and London: Harper and Brothers, 1925), p. 112.

# Bibliography

The bibliography lists most of the major writings of the authors who are examined in all chapters except the introductory one; included are several volumes that do not apply directly to the topic but illustrate distinctively the thought or method of their creator. A few titles clearly unrelated to the themes of the study or unnecessary to their demonstration have been omitted.

Anderson, Sherwood. *Beyond Desire.* New York: Liveright, 1932.

———. *Dark Laughter.* New York: Boni and Liveright, 1925.

———. *Death in the Woods and Other Stories.* New York: Liveright, 1933.

———. *Hello Towns!* New York: Liveright, 1929.

———. *Home Town.* New York: Alliance Book Corporation, 1940.

———. *Horses and Men: Tales, Long and Short, from Our American Life.* New York: B. W. Huebsch, 1923.

——. *Kit Brandon: A Portrait.* New York: Charles Scribner's Sons; London: Charles Scribner's Sons, Ltd., 1936.

——. *Letters of Sherwood Anderson.* Selected and edited with an introduction and notes by Howard Mumford Jones in association with Walter B. Rideout. Boston: Little, Brown and Company, 1953.

——. *Many Marriages.* New York: B. W. Huebsch, 1923.

——. *Marching Men.* New York: John Lane Company; London: John Lane; Toronto: S. B. Gundy, 1917.

——. *Mid-American Chants.* New York: John Lane Company; London: John Lane, 1918.

——. *The Modern Writer.* San Francisco: The Lantern Press, 1925.

——. *Nearer the Grass Roots, by Sherwood Anderson, and by the same author, an account of a journey—Elizabethton.* San Francisco: The Westgate Press, 1929.

——. *A New Testament.* New York: Boni and Liveright, 1927.

——. *No Swank.* Philadelphia: The Centaur Press, 1934.

——. *Perhaps Women.* New York: Liveright, 1931.

——. *Plays: Winesburg and Others.* New York: Charles Scribner's Sons; London: Charles Scribner's Sons, Ltd., 1937.

——. *Poor White.* New York: B. W. Huebsch, 1920.

——. *Puzzled America.* New York and London: Charles Scribner's Sons, 1935.

——. *Sherwood Anderson's Memoirs.* New York: Harcourt, Brace and Company, 1942.

——. *Sherwood Anderson's Notebook.* New York: Boni and Liveright, 1926.

——. *A Story Teller's Story.* New York: B. W. Huebsch, 1924.

——. *Tar: A Midwest Childhood.* New York: Boni and Liveright, 1926.

——. "The Times and the Towns." In *America as Americans See It.* Edited by Fred J. Ringel. New York: Harcourt, Brace and Company, 1932.

——. *The Triumph of the Egg: A Book of Impressions from American Life in Tales and Poems.* New York: B. W. Huebsch, 1921.

———. *Windy McPherson's Son.* New York: John Lane Company; London: John Lane, 1916.

———. *Winesburg, Ohio: A Group of Tales of Ohio Small Town Life.* New York: B. W. Huebsch, 1919.

Dos Passos, John. *Chosen Country.* Boston: Houghton Mifflin Company, 1951.

———. *District of Columbia.* Boston: Houghton Mifflin Company, 1952. Contains *Adventures of a Young Man* (1939), *Number One* (1943), and *The Grand Design* (1949).

———. *The Great Days.* New York: Sagamore Press, 1958.

———. *The Ground We Stand On: Some Examples from the History of a Political Creed.* New York: Harcourt, Brace and Company, 1941.

———. *The Head and Heart of Thomas Jefferson.* Garden City, N. Y.: Doubleday and Company, 1954.

———. *In All Countries.* New York: Harcourt, Brace and Company, 1934.

———. *Journeys Between Wars.* New York: Harcourt, Brace and Company, 1938.

———. *Manhattan Transfer.* New York and London: Harper and Brothers, 1925.

———. *The Men Who Made the Nation.* Garden City, N. Y.: Doubleday and Company, 1957.

———. *Midcentury.* Boston: Houghton Mifflin Company, 1961.

———. *Most Likely to Succeed.* New York: Prentice-Hall, 1954.

———. *One Man's Initiation—1917.* London: G. Allen and Unwin, 1920.

———. *Orient Express.* New York and London: Harper and Brothers, 1927.

———. "A Preface Twenty-Five Years Later." In *First Encounter*, a reissue of *One Man's Initiation—1917.* New York: Philosophical Library, 1945.

———. *The Prospect before Us.* Boston: Houghton Mifflin Company, 1950.

———. *Prospects of a Golden Age.* Englewood Cliffs, N. J.: Prentice-Hall, 1959.

———. *A Pushcart at the Curb*. New York: George H. Doran Company, 1922.

———. "Reminiscences of a Middle-Class Radical, II," *National Review*, I (February 15, 1956).

———. *Rosinante to the Road Again*. New York: George H. Doran Company, 1922.

———. *State of the Nation*. Boston: Houghton Mifflin Company, 1944.

———. *Streets of Night*. New York: George H. Doran Company, 1923.

———. *The Theme Is Freedom*. New York: Dodd, Mead and Company, 1956.

———. *Three Plays*. New York: Harcourt, Brace and Company, 1934. Contains "The Garbage Man" ["The Moon Is a Gong"] (1923), "Airways, Inc." (1928), and "Fortune Heights" (1933).

———. *Three Soldiers*. 1921. New York: Random House, The Modern Library, 1932.

———. *Tour of Duty*. Boston: Houghton Mifflin Company, 1946.

———. *U. S. A.* New York: Random House, The Modern Library, 1939. Contains *The 42nd Parallel* (1930), *Nineteen Nineteen* (1932), and *The Big Money* (1936).

Frank, Waldo. *America Hispana: A Portrait and a Prospect*. New York and London: Charles Scribner's Sons, 1931.

———. *The Bridegroom Cometh*. London: Victor Gollancz, 1938.

———. *Chalk Face*. New York: Boni and Liveright, 1924.

———. *Chart for Rough Water: Our Role in a New World*. New York: Doubleday, Doran and Company, 1940.

———. *City Block*. Darien, Conn.: Published by Waldo Frank, 1922.

———. *The Dark Mother*. New York: Boni and Liveright, 1920.

———. *Dawn in Russia: The Record of a Journey*. New York and London: Charles Scribner's Sons, 1932.

———. *The Death and Birth of David Markand: An American Story*. New York and London: Charles Scribner's Sons, 1934.

———. *Holiday*. New York: Boni and Liveright, 1923.

———. *In the American Jungle*. New York and Toronto: Farrar and Rinehart, 1937.

———. *The Invaders*. New York: Duell, Sloan and Pearce, 1948.

———. *Island in the Atlantic*. New York: Duell, Sloan and Pearce, 1946.

———. *Not Heaven: A Novel in the Form of Prelude, Variations, and Theme*. New York: Hermitage House, 1953.

———. *Our America*. New York: Boni and Liveright, 1919.

———. *Rahab*. New York: Boni and Liveright, 1922.

———. *The Re-discovery of America: An Introduction to a Philosophy of American Life*. New York and London: Charles Scribner's Sons, 1929.

———. *The Rediscovery of Man: A Memoir and a Methodology of Modern Life*. New York: George Braziller, 1958.

———. *Salvos: An Informal Book about Books and Plays*. New York: Boni and Liveright, 1924.

———. *Summer Never Ends: A Modern Love Story*. New York: Duell, Sloan and Pearce, 1941.

———. *The Unwelcome Man*. 1917. New York: Boni and Liveright, 1923.

Lewis, Sinclair. *Arrowsmith*. 1925. New York and Chicago: Harcourt, Brace and Company, 1945.

———. *Babbitt*. New York: Harcourt, Brace and Company, 1922.

———. "Be Brisk With Babbitt," *The Nation*, CXIX (October 15, 22, 29, 1924).

———. *Dodsworth*. New York: Harcourt, Brace and Company, 1929.

———. *Elmer Gantry*. New York: Harcourt, Brace and Company, 1927.

———. *From Main Street to Stockholm: Letters of Sinclair Lewis, 1919–1930*. Edited and with an introduction by Harrison Smith. New York: Harcourt, Brace and Company, 1952.

———. *It Can't Happen Here*. Garden City, N. Y.: Doubleday, Doran and Company, 1935.

———. *The Job: An American Novel*. New York and London: Harper and Brothers, 1917.

———. *Kingsblood Royal.* New York: Random House, 1947.

———. *Main Street: The Story of Carol Kennicott.* New York: Harcourt, Brace and Howe, 1920.

———. *The Man from Main Street. A Sinclair Lewis Reader. Selected Essays and Other Writings, 1904–1950.* Edited by Harry E. Maule and Melville H. Cane; assisted by Philip Allan Friedman. New York: Random House, 1953.

———. *The Man Who Knew Coolidge: Being the Soul of Lowell Schmaltz, Constructive and Nordic Citizen.* New York: Harcourt, Brace and Company, 1928.

———. *Our Mr. Wrenn: The Romantic Adventures of a Gentle Man.* New York and London: Harper and Brothers, 1914.

———. *The Prodigal Parents.* Garden City, N. Y.: Doubleday, Doran and Company, 1938.

———. *Selected Short Stories of Sinclair Lewis.* Garden City, N. Y.: Doubleday, Doran and Company, 1935.

———. "Self-Conscious America," *The American Mercury,* VI (October 1925).

———. *The Trail of the Hawk: A Comedy of the Seriousness of Life.* New York and London: Harper and Brothers, 1915.

———. *Work of Art.* Garden City, N. Y.: Doubleday, Doran and Company, 1934.

———. *World So Wide.* New York: Random House, 1951.

Mumford, Lewis. *Art and Technics.* New York: Columbia University Press, 1952.

———. *The Brown Decades: A Study of the Arts in America: 1865–1895.* New York: Harcourt, Brace and Company, 1931.

———. *The City in History: Its Origins, Its Transformations, and Its Prospects.* New York: Harcourt, Brace and World, 1961.

———. *The Condition of Man.* New York: Harcourt, Brace and Company, 1944.

———. *The Conduct of Life.* New York: Harcourt, Brace and Company, 1951.

———. *The Culture of Cities.* New York: Harcourt, Brace and Company, 1938.

———. *Faith for Living.* New York: Harcourt, Brace and Company, 1940.

———. *The Golden Day: A Study in American Experience and Culture*. New York: Boni and Liveright, 1926.

———. *Herman Melville*. New York: Harcourt, Brace and Company, 1929.

———. *In the Name of Sanity*. New York: Harcourt, Brace and Company, 1954.

———. *Men Must Act*. New York: Harcourt, Brace and Company, 1939.

———. *The South in Architecture: The Dancy Lectures, Alabama College, 1941*. New York: Harcourt, Brace and Company, 1941.

———. *Sticks and Stones: A Study of American Architecture and Civilization*. 1924. Second revised edition; New York: Dover Publications, 1955.

———. *The Story of Utopias*. Includes an introduction by Hendrik Willem Van Loon. New York: Boni and Liveright, 1922.

———. *Technics and Civilization*. New York: Harcourt, Brace and Company, 1934.

———. *The Transformations of Man*. New York: Harper and Brothers, 1956.

———. *Values for Survival: Essays, Addresses, and Letters on Politics and Education*. New York: Harcourt, Brace and Company, 1946.

Sandburg, Carl. *Complete Poems*. New York: Harcourt, Brace and Company, 1950.

———. *Remembrance Rock*. New York: Harcourt, Brace and Company, 1948.

Stearns, Harold. *America: A Re-appraisal*. New York: Hillman-Curl, 1937.

———. *America and the Young Intellectual*. New York: George H. Doran Company, 1921.

———. *America Now: An Inquiry into Civilization in the United States by Thirty-Six Americans*. Edited with an introduction by Harold E. Stearns. New York: Charles Scribner's Sons; London: Charles Scribner's Sons, Ltd., 1938.

———. *Civilization in the United States: An Inquiry by Thirty Americans*. Edited by Harold E. Stearns. New York: Harcourt, Brace and Company, 1922.

———. *Liberalism in America: Its Origin, Its Temporary Collapse, Its Future.* New York: Boni and Liveright, 1919.

———. *Rediscovering America.* New York: Liveright, 1934.

———. *The Street I Know.* New York: Lee Furman, 1935.

Veblen, Thorstein. *Absentee Ownership and Business Enterprise in Recent Times: The Case of America.* New York: B. W. Huebsch, 1923.

———. *The Engineers and the Price System.* New York: B. W. Huebsch, 1921.

———. *Essays in Our Changing Order.* Edited by Leon Ardzrooni. New York: The Viking Press, 1934.

———. *The Higher Learning in America: A Memorandum on the Conduct of Universities by Business Men.* New York: B. W. Huebsch, 1918.

———. *Imperial Germany and the Industrial Revolution.* New York: The Macmillan Company; London: Macmillan and Company, 1915.

———. *An Inquiry into the Nature of Peace and the Terms of Its Perpetuation.* New York: The Macmillan Company; London: Macmillan and Company, 1917.

———. *The Instinct of Workmanship and the State of the Industrial Arts.* New York: The Macmillan Company, 1914.

———. *The Place of Science in Modern Civilisation and Other Essays.* New York: B. W. Huebsch, 1919.

———. *The Theory of Business Enterprise.* New York: Charles Scribner's Sons, 1904.

———. *The Theory of the Leisure Class: An Economic Study in the Evolution of Institutions.* New York: The Macmillan Company; London: Macmillan and Company, 1899.

———. *The Vested Interests and the State of the Industrial Arts.* New York: B. W. Huebsch, 1919.

# *Additional References*

Several excellent interpretative works upon my authors are omitted because of the specialized nature of my topic and the limited and specialized use I have made of the reference readings.

Adams, Henry. *The Degradation of the Democratic Dogma.* With an introduction by Brooks Adams. 1919. New York: Capricorn Books, 1958. Contains "The Tendency of History" (1894), "A Letter to American Teachers of History" (1910), and "The Rule of Phase applied to History" (1909).

————. *The Education of Henry Adams: An Autobiography.* 1906. Boston and New York: Houghton Mifflin Company, 1946.

Bittner, William. *The Novels of Waldo Frank.* Philadelphia: University of Pennsylvania Press, 1958.

Carlyle, Thomas. "Chartism." 1839. In *The Works of Thomas Carlyle.* Centenary Edition; New York: Charles Scribner's Sons, 1898–1901. XXIX.

————. *On Heroes, Hero-Worship and the Heroic in History.* 1841. In *Works*, V.

————. *Past and Present.* 1843. In *Works*, X.

————. *Sartor Resartus.* 1833. In *Works*, I.

————. "Signs of the Times." 1829. In *Works*, XXVII.

Cowley, Malcolm. *Exile's Return: A Narrative of Ideas.* New York: W. W. Norton and Company, 1934.

Dickens, Charles. *Hard Times.* 1854. New York: Harper and Brothers, 1960. Includes an introduction by John H. Middendorf.

Eshleman, Lloyd Wendell. *A Victorian Rebel: The Life of William Morris.* New York: Charles Scribner's Sons, 1940.

Geismar, Maxwell. *Writers in Crisis: The American Novel: 1925–1940.* Boston: Houghton Mifflin Company, 1942.

Howe, Irving. *Sherwood Anderson.* New York: William Sloane Associates, 1951.

Kazin, Alfred. *On Native Grounds: An Interpretation of Modern American Prose Literature.* New York: Reynal and Hitchcock, 1942.

Marx, Karl. *Capital, the Communist Manifesto and Other Writings.* Edited with an introduction by Max Eastman. New York: Random House, The Modern Library, 1932.

Marx, Leo. *The Machine in the Garden: Technology and the Pastoral Ideal in America.* New York: Oxford University Press, 1964.

Riesman, David. *Thorstein Veblen: A Critical Interpretation.* New York: Charles Scribner's Sons; London: Charles Scribner's Sons, Ltd., 1953.

Rosenberg, Charles E. "Martin Arrowsmith: The Scientist as Hero," *American Quarterly*, XV (Fall 1963).

Ruskin, John. "The Nature of Gothic," from *The Stones of Venice*, II. 1853. New York: John Wiley and Sons, 1888.

————. *Unto This Last.* London: G. Allen and Unwin, 1923. The essays were first published in 1860.

Schevill, James. *Sherwood Anderson: His Life and Work.* Denver: The University of Denver Press, 1951.

Schorer, Mark. *Sinclair Lewis: An American Life.* New York,

Toronto, London: McGraw-Hill Book Company, 1961.

Van Doren, Carl. *The Nation*, CXLI (November 13, 1935).

Whipple, Thomas K. *Study Out the Land.* Berkeley and Los Angeles: University of California Press, 1943.

Whitman, Walt. *The Complete Poetry and Prose of Walt Whitman.* With an introduction by Malcolm Cowley. 2 vols. New York: Pellegrini and Cudahy, 1948.

Wrenn, John H. *John Dos Passos.* New York: Twayne Publishers, 1962.

# Index